Devil in Deerskins

Devil in Deerskins

My Life with Grey Owl

ANAHAREO

new press
TORONTO
1972

Design/Peter Maher

ISBN 0- 88770-126-4

new press

Editorial offices
84 Sussex Avenue
Toronto 179, Ontario

Order department
553 Richmond Street West
Toronto 133, Ontario

Manufactured in Canada
Printed by The Alger Press Limited,
Oshawa, Ontario

Foreword

More than three decades have passed since the death of Grey Owl, one of the most colorful and controversial people to walk across the Canadian stage. His name, internationally known in the thirties, should not be forgotten, and it is gratifying that the lady who is best able to tell the Grey Owl story is now placing it on permanent record.

The name of Grey Owl will have different meanings for different people. For some it will bring memories of a tall, lean Englishman, Archie Belaney, who, with moccasins, long hair and buckskin clothing, succeeded in passing without question as a North American Indian and winning international attention. To others, the name will suggest mainly a naturalist who projected his beaver, McGinty and McGinnis, Jellyroll and Rawhide, to fame. And to still others the name will always recall the trapper who was converted to a genuine feeling for wildlife and became one of the most dedicated of conservationists.

The revelation of Grey Owl's true background and original name brought widespread surprise and interest. But what was more important by far was the message brought to Canadians and others of wild things having rights and deserving to be treated with compassion. He had been a trapper but thanks to the influence of Anahareo, the creator of this book, he abandoned trapping and all needless killing. 'I realized,' he

v

wrote, 'what a crime we trappers were committing against nature that had been so bountiful. I dedicated my life at that moment to conservation of game.' The wild creatures became his friends, and he found an unusual talent for communicating with them. They seemed to trust him and he did not fail them.

He disliked zoos, in which freedom-loving animals were given life sentences in dirty little cages and pens. 'The saddest place in any city,' he wrote, 'is the animal park.' His anger was aroused when in an English park he found a beaver without a mate, without a pond bigger than a bathtub, and without vegetation except what was cut and thrown over the fence.

Grey Owl wrote numerous books and articles, all pleading for understanding and conservation of wildlife. He related very little about himself but he did acknowledge that the inspiration to change from 'a bloody trapper to a brother of the beaver people' came from the lady whose story Canadians should now be eager to read.

In many ways, Grey Owl was years ahead of his time. At his period in Canadian history, conservation was not a popular topic. Were he living today, he would find many more sympathetic listeners when he talked about the wilderness and its denizens.

It is a matter of the highest personal gratification that Grey Owl will return in the pages of *Devil in Deerskins*.

GRANT MACEWAN

Acknowledgments

Acknowledgment is made for the excerpt from *The Men of the Last Frontier* by Grey Owl, by permission of The Macmillan Company of Canada Limited, and to Peter Davies Limited, London, who hold the British rights to *The Men of the Last Frontier*.

To my daughter Dawn

Devil in Deerskins

It was the Moon of the Windigo and the tamarack, sounding like rifle fire, cracked in the freezing night. The little black spruce were hunched and distorted, bent to the breaking point under their burden of snow. This was northern Quebec in midwinter, at midnight, and well below zero.

Unaccustomed to snowshoeing, I trudged on as if in a dream – a nightmare to be more precise – for ahead of me was this stranger. It disgusted me to see him swinging along as if on a wafting breeze, hauling a toboggan with its 150-pound load, while I staggered desperately to keep up.

After twenty weary miles, I realized what an imbecile I had been to come – now there was no turning back. So I struggled on and cursed my stupidity for accepting his invitation.

Following the toboggan as it snaked over and around the humps and bumps of the trail, my thoughts flew back to a warm, sunny afternoon six months earlier.

It was late in the summer of 1925 and I was at Wabikon, a resort on Lake Temagami. I was reading in the shade of the pines, when I was interrupted by a gritting sound from the beach. Looking up to find the source of the disturbance, I saw a man dressed in brown deerskins stepping with the speed and grace of a panther from a canoe. And there he stood, tall, straight, and handsome, gazing wistfully across the lake in the direction from which he had come. As he stood there with his paddle in his hand, his attitude seemed to express such yearning and loneliness that my heart quite went out to him. However, since I was young and scatterbrained, the mental or spiritual attitude of people didn't interest me for long and, unseen by him, I immediately began to take stock of this most striking man's appearance.

His shirt and trousers were dark brown, brightened by a Hudson's Bay belt and a much worn buckskin vest, which matched the moccasins on his feet. But what really set my imagination afire was his long hair and wide-brimmed hat. This was the first time that I set eyes on Archie Belaney, Englishman, trapper, and guide – later known as Grey Owl, author, lecturer, and naturalist – Brother of the Beaver People. In my imagination, this man looked like the ever so thrilling hero of my youth, Jesse James, that mad, dashing, and romantic Robin Hood of America.

From my vantage point I saw Grey Owl ease the canoe farther onto shore, and then he walked up the trail to the office. My book forgotten, I waited for his return. Then, with bated breath I watched my Jesse James walk down the trail, step into the canoe, and paddle away. I felt a distinct pang of sadness.

My curiosity thoroughly aroused, I hurried to the office to ask who he was. The manager of the resort told me that his name was Archie Belaney and that they had just hired him as a guide. I was delighted. I also found out that he preferred his tent to the guide's quarters and was camping a short distance up the lake, and that he would have his meals in the staff dining-room. So, around suppertime I went to a long rustic bench under the pines, where he had to pass. However, I needn't have knocked myself out trying to get to know him, because when he first saw me he stopped short in his tracks and stared, un-abashed, till I wished the earth would swallow me up. Then, with a serious stone-faced expression, he came and asked, 'Say, do you happen to have a bag of potatoes?'

Now, anything connected with this Godlike male, whose proud and masterful appearance struck my very soul with awe, simply could not be ridiculous, and I took him to be in dead earnest. When I stuttered something about not having any

2

potatoes he said, 'That's all right, you'd likely not have the kind of potatoes I like anyhow.'

'Then what kind of potatoes do you like?' I asked.

'Those eyeless ones,' he answered, with a teasing glint in his eye. I walked away angry and disillusioned.

He seemed to be under the impression that the best way to win friends and influence nineteen-year-old girls was to be annoying – he had a way of creating an embarrassing situation and then leaving you holding the bag. For instance, I was deeply engrossed in a book when suddenly I was startled by the sudden shifting and creaking of the old bench. I looked up quickly and there sat Grey Owl holding on to the bench for dear life.

'I wish you wouldn't rock the boat like that,' he gasped.

'But I didn't!' I exclaimed.

'It certainly wasn't me,' he said, exuding innocence.

'Say, are you crazy or something?'

'Now you're mad,' he said, feigning regret.

I turned back to my book but of course couldn't concentrate. What a dope, I thought.

He shook the bench again, but this time I wasn't going to pay any attention. Undiscouraged by this lack of response, he commenced flailing his arms around as if beating off a swarm of hornets.

'There it goes again – why do you insist?'

'I was here first and I have every right . . . .' I began, but wasn't allowed to finish.

'Ah, your rights, yes of course, your rights,' he interrupted in mock sympathy, and then wrinkling his brow as if in great concentration continued, 'If I remember correctly – in 1835, somebody did something about equal rights – oh skip it, it was a flop anyway.'

I closed my book with a bang, got up and left him sitting there. I had gone only a few paces when I turned and was about to say 'I hope you're satisfied' or something equally smart and original, but was stopped by his hateful, teasing grin.

Our next encounter was that same night at the dance at Bear Island, six miles away. The dance was in full swing when our crowd, the Wabikon gang, arrived. The lively orchestra consisted of an accordion, piano, fiddle, and drum, and there at the drum sat none other than A. Belaney.

I was rather proud of my New Yorker escort in plus fours and lemonade shirt, and steering him towards the orchestra I threw a careless grin at Archie. He immediately put down the drumsticks, gave me an icy look, and left the hall.

After the dance, as we were all straggling down to the boats and canoes, Archie appeared out of nowhere, grabbed me by the arm, whisked me aside, and whispered, 'Can't you do any better than that dissipated-looking so-and-so?' This reference to my escort made me furious, and drawing myself up in a huff I said, 'Fred is perfectly O.K., and that is good enough for me.'

'Ah, he might be good enough for some people,' Archie growled, 'but if I had a sister I'd wring her neck . . . .'

I heard no more; I was well on my way to the lake.

A few days after, he was away on a fishing trip when I received a wire telling me that Natalie, my little five-year-old niece, had died. I left immediately without seeing him again, and although he was often in my thoughts, affairs at home in Mattawa occupied all my time. Home was a frame house by a stand of white pine where I lived with my widowed father and a brother and sister. My father was a trapper, guide, carpenter, logger and river driver – he was ninety-nine when he died.

After Natalie's funeral, Father seemed so heartbroken I decided to remain at home, but after the carefree days at Wabikon, my own home, saddened with grief, seemed quiet and gloomy. As the days passed, I began to think more and more of the man who, in my few encounters with him, had left me in such a boiling temper. I told myself that if he could only see me in my own home, he would have more respect for me than he had so far shown, and the urge to write and invite him down finally won out. I knew it would take three days for my letter to reach him, so you can imagine my surprise when I saw him walking through our gate the day after I had mailed the letter.

Hidden behind the curtains, I watched him. He closed the gate with unnecessary care and turned slowly around. He seemed undecided; then suddenly he straightened up, looking much taller than his six foot two, and with chin jutting out walked with great determination to the door. When I let him in, I noticed with relief that he bore no trace of his former manner. Instead he was shy and quite uncertain of himself, but charming, I thought, for all that.

After the exchange of numerous smiles, he finally got up enough courage to talk. 'I wrote you and told you I was coming, but I guess I got on the same train, being it was there – sort of,' he said, smiling apologetically.

That was rather involved, but I got what he meant and confessed writing him an invitation. This restored his self-confidence considerably. Quite considerably in fact, because soon we were quarrelling again. He never meant to be sarcastic, but his opinions simply had to be aired, and his opinion on this occasion concerned my dress.

'Don't you think that you wear your skirts a little too short?' he asked critically.

I tried to keep calm, but without success. I told him that my skirt was not too short and on looking him over, continued. 'Since you are so clothes-conscious, why are you wrapped in that awful oilskin? It isn't raining you know.'

For answer, he flipped his coat open and revealed a revolver hanging from his hip. I swallowed twice in my excitement – not fear or apprehension; somehow I just couldn't keep my eyes off the revolver. He answered my queries by simply saying, 'Everything is O.K. but the gun is necessary. I'll explain sometime.' This evasive answer only succeeded in arousing my curiosity and hence more questions, so after much coaxing he agreed to fill in the details.

'One day, just for fun I was throwing a knife and accidentally cut a guy – 'course the police came after me, but when they found out that it was an accident, they said it was O.K.'

What really happened, I learned much later when Archie and a fellow trapper were rehashing old times in Bisco [Biscotasing]:

Archie made his headquarters in Bisco before and after the First World War. When he came back from overseas he was drawing full pension, which gives you an idea of the state of his health at that time. He had been in a gas attack and had shrapnel in his foot. As a badly wounded soldier with little hope of recovering, he faced a futile and unhappy existence. He became dispirited and gloomy and turned to music for solace. He used to buy records by the dozen and take them to a friend's home to sit in the darkened parlour with his special brand of scotch and his memories, listening to music by the hour.

One afternoon this procedure was interrupted by the tearful voice of a very excited young girl. She had arrived home late from school, and her mother was preparing to give her a spanking. The girl, crying frantically, said that the other girls had coaxed her to go to 'Joe's place' and that Joe wouldn't let her leave.

That was sufficient to move Archie, who knew something of Joe's character. Moving with that silent speed that I came to know so well, he collected a half-dozen or so of his knives – he always had several well balanced throwing knives – and went to throw a scare into Joe.

Once inside Joe's place, and seizing the man himself, he came right to the point and accused Joe of the worst in regard to the girl. Joe denied it, but Archie told him that there was going to be no fooling around, and if he didn't come clean he would disembowel him and drop his guts on the floor. Archie said that he would give him one chance to tell the truth, and Joe took that chance. The truth only made Archie more furious.

'Stand with your back against the door,' Archie commanded, but the man, crying, said, 'No, no, Archie.'

'Do as I say,' said Archie, playing the role to the hilt.

'Please don't kill me!' the man begged, backing to the door.

'No, I don't intend to kill you, Joe,' Archie replied, as he slowly examined the blades and balance of his knives, prolonging the man's anguish. 'Oh hell, here's one that's no damn good. Have you got a file, Joe?'

'No,' screamed Joe.

'O.K. then, let's get on with it,' said Archie in a businesslike manner. Joe, paralyzed with fright, could only shake his head in the negative.

'Stand still, Joe, or you might get hurt!' Archie warned, and then said, as he raised the knife in readiness, 'I've got a queer quirk too, Joe.' Zing went the knife.

The man kept saying, 'Please don't . . . please don't!'

'I'll let you in on a secret, Joe.' He let go of another knife. 'I've always loved live targets, Joe.' The third knife zinged through the air. This was more than Joe could take, and he moved his arm as if to ward off the knife. This was a mistake, as it struck him in the hand. At the sight of the blood spurting out of his hand, Joe wheeled frantically out of the shack and went straight to the police, while Archie just stood by in surprise until it dawned on him that an attempted-murder charge could be pretty uncomfortable.

He hurried over to his Indian friend, Alex, and told him of his predicament. Between them they arranged an immediate exit from town, and when Archie was established on the top of a bald hill overlooking Bisco, Alex went back to town to find out what course the law was going to take. After dark that night Alex came back, flushed with excitement, and told Archie not to show himself, as the police from the west had come in on the night train to get him. That was bad news.

Archie had to spend several cold days and nights, for he didn't dare make a fire. In the meantime, the townspeople protested at having Archie penalized for what he had done to Joe, and the school trustees put the case to the police. They decided they didn't want Archie too badly after all, and left town. Alex lost no time in delivering the good news to Archie.

On his return to Bisco, everyone welcomed him back, congratulated him, and even held a dance in honour of the fugitive that very night. However, during the celebrations the town constable told Archie that if he ever got into trouble with the law, the attempted-murder charge would be thrown in.

'Oh,' I sighed, 'I sure wish I could throw a knife.' Silence. 'And I wish I was a good shot too,' I said.

Silence again. 'Are you going to shoot somebody with that?' I wanted to know, pointing at the gun. He gave me a startled look and said, 'Of course not'.

'Then why are you carrying it?' I persisted, a little disappointed. With thinning patience he explained. 'This thing is used only to divert attention long enough for me to get away.'

'To get away from what?' I asked.

'The police,' he answered abruptly.

My excitement mounting, I asked, 'Are they after you again?'

'No,' he answered shortly.

I didn't believe him and said, 'You can tell me, you know. I'll never tell anybody.'

7

He gathered from my attitude that I was thinking he had done something terrible, and he was right; that is exactly what I was thinking. By way of straightening me out, he said, 'I took a chance on coming down here by train – I could have been spotted.'

'So what?' I asked lightly.

'So what!' he repeated with astonishment.

'Yeah, so what.'

'Well, if you think I'm going to just stand by while they slap an attempted-murder charge on me . . . .'

'But you've just told me that everything was O.K.,' I interrupted.

'Not exactly,' Archie said, calming down somewhat. 'You see, I was told that this thing could come up if I did anything again.'

'Oh heck, you've got nothing to worry about.' Then an exciting thought struck me, and I added teasingly, 'Oh, oh, Archie, did you do something again?'

'Well, if you must know,' he said, exasperated beyond measure, 'I slugged the station agent at Bisco.'

I loved this and was enthusiastic at the prospect of more blood and thunder. Noticing this, Archie, with not a little sarcasm added, 'I'm sorry I didn't kill the guy because I know how much you would have enjoyed that.'

I ignored this. What he had done wasn't so bad in itself – he merely gave the station agent a couple of swings (which happened to connect) for not delivering his telegram. It had concerned some sportsmen from New York whom Archie was to guide on a six-week trip. The agent had wanted Archie to miss this job and deliberately withheld the wire. Anyway, Archie had hit an official who was on duty and that meant trouble with the authorities.

The attempted-murder charge had reared its ugly head again and sent Archie on his way, and now here he was at my home, peeling potatoes, for suppertime had slipped around much too quickly and my father would soon be home.

Archie and I were getting along exceedingly well for a change, so the time passed quickly and pleasantly, and when my father came in, the meal was waiting. Introductions were informal. They exchanged a firm handshake, and then Archie and Papa were getting along like old friends. They talked about all the places they had been, though at different times. They exchanged stories and experiences, the notorious rapids they had conquered, trapping and methods of setting traps for various animals, everything about the bush.

At supper Papa said, 'My daughter hasn't told me anything about you. I don't even know where you are from.'

Archie said that he trapped out of Bisco and was now moving on. Papa enquired, 'Are your parents still living there?'

'No, my folks are dead,' Archie answered shortly.

'Well, that's too bad,' Papa said. 'I'm sorry to hear that. I've never been to Bisco.'

'Is that where you were born?' I asked.

'No,' said Archie, uncomfortable under my father's expectant gaze. Papa sensed this and quickly changed the subject. It was obvious from his evasion and clipped answers that Archie would just as soon drop the subject, but I, crass and immature, didn't let it go at that, and asked, 'Well then, where were you born?' Papa gave me a disapproving look.

'I come from Mexico,' answered Archie.

Papa looked interested and I, in great excitement, asked, 'Then you're Mexican?'

'No, my father was Scotch and my mother was an Apache Indian.'

Papa said 'Aha, I thought you looked Indian, but with your blue eyes, I didn't know. I'm Iroquois, but my grandmother was Scotch. She was captured by my people a long time ago. Her name was Mary Robinson. Oh, it's a long story.' He shrugged, then asked, 'How is trapping in Bisco these days?'

This started the conversational ball rolling again. They were back in their element, so much so that after four hours of this I left, knowing that I wouldn't be missed. I knew too that Papa would be keeping Archie for the night, so I remained at my cousins'.

Thinking how well Archie and I had managed to get along during the latter part of his visit, my anticipation and spirits were high as I entered the gate to our home the next day. My exhilaration was short-lived, however, for the first thing I saw was the two men shaking hands in the doorway, so I knew Archie must be leaving. I rushed up to them and asked, 'You aren't leaving, are you?' Stupid question when it was obvious that he was.

I was disappointed, and Archie, detecting this, smiled at my concern and said something to the effect that had he been in his right mind he would by now have been on his way into his hunting ground. This was a gibe at my leaving the night before.

'Aaaah, stay for another day?' I coaxed.

'Thank you, but the answer is no.'

'Then I'll walk to the train with you.'

'As you like,' Archie answered stonily, and he waved farewell to my father. Turning to me he said, 'We'll walk down the railroad track.'

We walked in silence, and I remember thinking that it was lucky it was raining because he was wearing that awful yellow oilskin coat again. At last Archie broke the silence to ask, somewhat ominously, 'Where in hell were you last night?'

'At my cousins'. Didn't my father tell you?'

'I didn't ask.'

We walked on without another word. Then I said, 'I'll be going to a convent next month.'

In shocked disbelief, Archie turned to me and all but shouted 'Are you out of your mind?'

'No.'

'Then just where did you get that crazy idea?'

I told him about Dr. Howard, from New York, who was thirty-four, tall and handsome. I had met him at Wabikon when he was up on a three-week vacation. We had such fun together, fishing, swimming, lunching out, and exploring the islands. He was an accomplished artist and I used to watch in fascination as he sketched or painted. He did a likeness of me once, which I thought was great; not only the picture, but being 'done' in oils. To make a long story short, Dr. Jim, as I came to call him, thought, for no obvious reason, that I had the brains worthy of an education and offered to pay my tuition to any school, college, or convent for as long as I wanted to continue my studies. My father and I thought this the opportunity of a lifetime and were most appreciative, but my father made the stipulation that it should be a Canadian school.

What with the writing back and forth, answering Papa's questions, it took quite some time before the final decision was made, but eventually I received a letter from Dr. Jim, who had returned to New York, telling me that he was in contact with the Loretto Abbey in Toronto and asking if that would be all right. It appeared that I was on my way to higher learning, the protégé of a fine New York doctor. I was awaiting the final arrangements when Archie came to visit.

'Remember this,' Archie said seriously, after a long silence. 'If ever you want to escape from the convent, just let me know and I'll get the gang from Bisco. You can bet your bottom dollar we'll get you out of there in no time flat.'

'Oh, thank you, thank you, I'll certainly remember that,' I assured him. How terribly thrilled I was at the prospect of being rescued by the Bisco Gang!

'Dr. Jim,' I continued, 'said that if I progressed satisfactorily in my studies he would treat me to a trip to Europe next summer, and that I could choose my own companion and . . . '

'Say, how old is this doctor?' Archie interrupted.

'Thirty-four.'

'Oh, is that so – the whole thing sounds pretty fishy to me.'

Not understanding the reference I smiled and said something about how interesting it would be to see the Pope!

We were still some distance from the station when I heard the train pulling in, and I automatically hastened my step, but Archie took my arm and said, 'This will be good enough.'

'What do you mean?' I asked.

'I'll hop on here . . . to avoid the crowd, you know.'

His meaning was quite clear so I stood by his side, worried, and hoping that he wouldn't be caught. The train stopped and stayed but a minute in the little town, and it was soon coming our way slowly, still working up steam. We shook hands and said good-bye, but just before he made a dash for the moving train, he said, 'Hey Reptile, I'll be seein' you whether you like it or not. . . .'

I wondered why he hadn't kissed me – not that I wanted him to love me. I just thought I was irresistable.

I received a letter every day for two weeks after Archie's departure, then suddenly they stopped. For five months there wasn't a word from him. If only I had not lost those letters, I would put them down here, and without a doubt they would be the better part of this book. They were all ninety or more pages

– one was a hundred and four pages – and they were all interesting and imaginative. When a letter came from Archie, my brother Eddie would drape himself over my shoulder and read without my permission, and so absorbing were the narratives, he would urge me to hurry if I happened to be a little too slow in turning pages to suit him.

In the meantime I had received word from Loretto Abbey telling me I would have to wait until the beginning of the next term to enrol. I wrote to Archie about this and the five-month-long silence was broken, not by letter but by telegram and a return ticket. The wire read 'Please come up for a day or more. Reply Yes.'

I didn't know what to do. I certainly wanted to go, but something held me back, so I asked my brother his opinion. He said, 'Sure, he seems like a heck of a good guy, and it would be a nice trip.' My sister, of course, shook her head and said, 'Certainly not!' She detested Archie's bushwhacker clothes and long hair, and, of course, she thought his yellow oilskins awful.

My father was only seven miles away finishing a country school that he had contracted to build. 'That would be only a fourteen-mile walk,' I thought bravely, never having walked that distance before. I started early and walked the seven miles to my father in a relatively short time. Papa stalled at first, but when I said I would be back for certain in a week, he relented, saying, 'All right, but take care of yourself, and be a good girl.' Though he always called Archie the 'Wendigo', my father liked Archie.

In February 1926, I started the journey by train to Forsythe in northern Quebec, where Archie was to meet me. After thirty-eight hours in the stuffy coach, I was overjoyed when the conductor came with the news that we had arrived. I gathered my things and followed him down the aisle to the door, and there in the moonlight night I was dumped off, as it were, onto a snowbank. There wasn't a soul in sight! Filled with consternation, I looked about and saw only four or five houses, all in darkness except one. There wasn't even a station, just a snowbank and I was on it, and alone.

Happily, as the last coach passed by, I heard a voice shout, 'Stay where you are, I'll be with you.' It was Archie! I slid off my perch and ran to him. He greeted me with a firm handshake, and we were unduly happy to see each other, considering that we had been in each other's company for only a matter of nine or ten hours up till then. Of course, through his letters I felt that I had known him for a much longer time. So I gave myself over to his care without a thought.

As the sound of the train faded in the distance, the strains of a lively tune came to us from a lamp-lit house, which we were now approaching, and where Archie had previously arranged for me to stay – the home of Mr. and Mrs. Henri. At the door we stopped and listened. Someone was playing 'Life in the Finland Woods' on an accordion.

Archie took this opportunity to tell me that there were four families in Forsythe; the men worked for the railroad as maintenance men. Mr. Henri was foreman. They were a very hospitable people and because of this and their isolated existence they craved company. No matter who, whether they were fur traders, prospectors, trappers, or Indians, they simply had to stay over and have a party. 'There are three trappers in there right now. That's one of them playing the accordion.'

We entered as soon as the music stopped and I was warmly greeted by the total population of Forsythe. The introductions over, I tidied up, ate supper, answered a thousand and one questions, and got acquainted. Then Mr. Henri got the ball rolling by suggesting a quadrille. So, to an orchestra consisting of a fiddle, a guitar, and an accordion, we danced all the old-time dances till morning. The next night we went to another house and did the same thing. It was around 4 a.m. when we returned to the Henris'. After a lively post-mortem on the party, the Henris and the trappers left Archie and me in the kitchen, and they went off to bed.

With a house full of people, Archie and I had never been alone. Now that we were, one would think that we would have had a lot to say, but after they had gone we fell silent. I was thinking, regretfully, that I had but one more day left on my visit. (When I'd promised my father that I would be back in a week, I hadn't known that travelling time would be a day and a half.) 'Why so glum?' asked Archie.

'Oh, I was just thinking how I hate the thought of leaving these people . . . but tomorrow I guess, it's good-bye.' I was about to add that I was sorry too to be leaving him, when he cut in with, 'I can't say that I'm sorry to hear that, because I've been away from my traps much too long as it is.'

This hit me like a wet towel. His telegram had stated in box-car letters to come for a day or more, and now here he was complaining about my wasting too much of his time – or something to that effect. Hurt and indignant, I said I was sorry for having overstayed my welcome.

'What? Where did you get that silly idea?' he asked.

'From you. You've just said that.'

'I did not!'

'But you did. Let me remind you that in your own words you said that you weren't sorry that I was leaving.'

'Let's get this straight.'

'You really don't have to make any excuses.'

'Say, listen,' he said, shaking me by the shoulders. 'How could you possibly overstay a visit you haven't even started – don't you understand?'

Of course I didn't, but said nothing. So he went on, 'That telegram meant that you were to come into my trapping grounds for a day or more with me!'

The idea was impossible, but I was glad that I hadn't made myself too obvious for too long. When I told him that my going into the bush with him was out of the question, he said, after what seemed an endless silence, 'Yeah, I guess it was a hare-brained notion after all. Put it down to wishful thinking. You know when a man is alone in the bush and he happens to get an idea, whether it is a good one or not, there's never anyone around to laugh him out of it. That's about it.'

The prospect of going into the north with a real live Jesse James had set my imagination afire, and I would have gone with Archie without a qualm if it hadn't been for the worry it would cause my father. Even so, the devil in me persisted, and I said, 'If I did go with you, could we be back in a week?'

'Sure, easily,' Archie answered, brightening.

'I'd sure like to take that trip with you, but . . . .'

'But, what? Are you afraid of me?'

'Of course not.'

14

'Then what's holding you back?'

'It's my father, he'd worry something awful. But let's write and explain that I had misunderstood your telegram.'

'We can do better than that, we'll phone him.'

Unfortunately, like the men in Forsythe, the phone was a railroader too, and it just wouldn't work for us. So we wrote to my father and told him that I was going into the bush for a week. Also, that I was having a wonderful time and not to worry, and Archie told him he would bring me back safe and sound, etc. The letter finished, we said good-night.

When I awakened at noon, I was surprised to find that Archie had already been to Doucet and back, a total of fourteen miles. He'd gone there to see a man about taking me into Archie's camp by dog-team. The man was to come early the following morning. After lunch Archie presented me with a pair of buckskin mitts and moccasins, and a stack of hefty woollen socks, long johns, and a pair of snowshoes decorated with red and green pompoms. Real sharp.

By mid-morning the following day, Archie was fit to be tied, for the man hadn't come with the dogs. At last Archie said, 'Let's walk in and take it easy.'

'Sure, let's.' Since we had been ready and waiting for hours, we had only to slip into the snowshoe bridles and we were set to go. 'Good-bye Mrs. Henri . . . see you in a week.' I waved as I followed the overloaded toboggan that Archie was hauling.

How excited and gay (and ignorant) I was when we started out that bright and frosty morning. 'How far?' I asked. 'Not very,' said he, and that terminated any further discussion as far as Archie was concerned; from then on all my questions and remarks were acknowledged by a variation of grunts. However, in spite of – or because of – this, I kept right on talking. Finally he turned and said, 'You'd better save that energy for the trail.'

Shut up, in other words.

It was becoming quite clear that this outing was not going to be the fun that I had expected it to be. I cut the chatter, but what energy I'd saved by not talking, I burnt up in anger, which I was to regret, for after five hours of snowshoeing I was all but crawling on my eyebrows. I was exhausted, but there was nary a word – let alone one of sympathy – from my travelling companion. Travelling companion? By this time I was thinking of Archie in far less flattering terms.

I began to realize what a fool I'd been to come. Which was the real Archie, I wondered. Was he the Archie I had come to like and trust, or this – sadist? What would become of me? Horrible thoughts closed in, and I worked myself into a fine lather of fear.

Finally the toboggan ceased its grinding moan over the frozen snow. We had come to a halt, and the man said, 'Ha, we are half way!' Half way? Why, I'd been hoping to sight the cabin for the last six miles. The man unhitched himself from the toboggan and got a pack-sack from the load. 'It's time for lunch,' he said, and went about knocking snow off a fallen tree, making a place for us to sit. 'Come,' he invited. Then, settling himself beside me, he separated several slices of frozen bannock and gave one to me. It felt like a chip of ice. 'Have you got some snow on your bannock?' he asked, as he passed the sugar.

'No, no snow,' I answered.

'Then put some on.'

'Why?' I asked, not caring especially.

'It keeps the sugar from sliding off.' A snow and sugar sandwich! What next?

Archie made a few attempts at conversation, but I was too angry and tired to answer. Sensing my mood, he sat in contented silence, as he preferred not to 'jabber' – as he called it – on the trail anyhow.

We started on again when the moon rose above the trees, stopping occasionally to eat a handful of dried apples and a fistful of snow. I envied him his endurance, for he was still going strong in spite of his 150-pound load. Some million hours later, the trek came to a halt, and thinking it was just another dried-apple time, I lurched towards the load to rest.

'We're home – welcome to Sunset Lodge!' Archie said triumphantly. He sounded almost human.

'Are we really here?' I asked.

'Yeah, we're here,' he answered.

I looked about and asked 'Where?'

'There,' he said, pointing.

I looked where he indicated, but saw nothing except three feet of tent protruding from a mound of snow, and a skinny stove-pipe poking through at one side. I was too tired to care. Forty miles is a long distance to one unaccustomed to snow-shoeing. I watched numbly as he shovelled a path to the mound with his snowshoe. I noticed that when he stood up, the ridge-pole or roof barely came to his waist, and I vaguely wondered how one could possibly live in a place like that. Suddenly he wasn't there! He'd disappeared in the snow – but even that didn't faze me. Then a light appeared in a yard-square aperture. 'Come in,' he called. Like an automaton I did as he said. I even tried to enter with snowshoes on. He thought this wildly funny. 'Ha, ha, ha . . . you'd better take them off! Ha, ha.'

What a jolly fellow, I thought angrily. I crawled through the opening and would have dropped the four feet to the floor if Archie hadn't caught me.

'Ha, ha, ha,' he howled again.

I was astonished that one could stand and still have plenty of head space to the ridge-pole. I noted that every inch of the ceiling was coated with hoar frost, as were the log walls. It was a veritable snow-house. Archie was busy making a fire in one of the smallest stoves I'd ever seen, and I just stood, drooping, watching the candle flicker and sputter in the drafty dug-out. My tired eyes roved over the interior, and I gasped something about its not having any windows. Then I reeled towards the bunk and there I sprawled. 'I'm going to stay right here for a week . . . maybe months,' I mumbled and knew no more.

Dear old Sunset Lodge. With that name you would naturally visualize a huge, rambling bungalow with annexes galore, ver-andahs, and sunporches, but Sunset Lodge was just a hole in the snow.

I don't know how long I'd slept, when Archie awakened me. It was evening, for the candle was lit. Archie offered me a steaming bowl of tea. I looked about with a clearer eye, and nearly panicked at what I saw. Above me was a canvas roof, mildewed and grey with age; there were no windows; the walls were constructed of logs, and the top one was covered with frost. There was a pole floor, and even the surface of the table was made of spruce poles about two inches in diameter, and had humps and bumps the size of the Rockies. What had I got myself into? However, the place was warm; and, comforted by the thought that I would be leaving in four days, I found that I was hungry and that I needed to go to the bathroom. When I asked where, Archie replied, 'Outside.' Where else?

By the time I'd washed and tidied up, supper was on the table. Archie was in great form. He talked, he laughed and joked, as we ate moose meat and raisin pancakes. Ah, but his beaming smile and joviality didn't fool me, for I remembered all too well his cold and unsympathetic attitudes towards me on the trip in. I was excruciatingly polite during supper, but didn't rise to his fun and games, and he, of course, knew the reason. He apologized, saying, 'I'm really sorry about how I acted on the trail, but I had to know if you had the guts that I hoped you had. I wanted to see what kind of stuff you were made of. . . . I was putting you to the test.' This made me angry, so I ate my pancake in silence.

'Have another?' he asked.

'No thanks.'

'You don't know how lucky you are.'

'Lucky?' I asked.

'In case you are not aware, I never, never put raisins in my pancakes for just anybody,' he said, affecting a haughty manner. He was just putting me on.

After supper, Archie handed me my parka and said, 'Come on, kid, I have a surprise for you.'

We climbed out of the opening and stood up. Archie said, pointing, 'There is your surprise; from me to you.'

I could see the outline of a cabin in the moonlight, and he led me to it. Above the door, written in black canoe pitch, was PONY HALL. I was delighted with this, as Pony was a nickname given me by my father. I swung the door wide and was thrilled with what I saw. The log walls, the bark still intact, were chinked with red, green, and yellow moss. It looked like rich tapestry, puffing out row upon row between the dark green logs. Even the windows sported this same type of chinking, the glass surrounded by lacy moss, a beautiful and unique frame. The small table was covered with bright new oilcloth. The chairs were blocks of wood, about a foot and a half in diameter. The shining hair of the moose-hide rug reflected shafts of light from the noisy fire in the little stove, and the bunk was fluffed high with balsam boughs covered by a red Hudson's Bay blanket. It was the ultimate in charm – and I loved it.

Satisfied that his surprise was duly appreciated, Archie left me there and busied himself moving everything but his own personal effects from Sunset Lodge to Pony Hall. When he'd dumped the last load he said, 'Well kid, I'll have to shake a leg and get my things ready for tomorrow. I'll be gone for a few days.'

Shocked, I asked, 'Where are you going?'

'To see my traps. If you're going to leave in a week, we'll have to get some cash in here pretty quick.' Wrinkling his forehead, he added, 'I've sure reneged on the job this winter.'

Terrified of being left by myself, I said, 'But you can't leave me here alone!'

Surprised, Archie asked 'Why not?'

'Why?' I screeched. 'Because I have never been in the bush by myself before. That's why.'

Archie, more than puzzled, said quietly, 'I can't imagine you being scared of anything, much less of just being by yourself.'

Naturally he was puzzled. I never walked – I swaggered. I was nineteen-year-old arrogance personified, and I always put on a bold, brave front. I'd been caught off guard, and my fear was showing. I was scared, but I was now more ashamed than anything else and said, 'Oh, I'm not scared, never think that. I was only thinking what a queer way to treat a guest – bringing me here and then dropping me right in the middle of nowhere, just like that!' I snapped my fingers at him for emphasis.

Archie grinned. 'Good kid! That's the stuff. I knew all along that you weren't afraid. I'm sorry I mentioned it.'

I was furious. I knew that I hadn't fooled him one little bit.

Archie returned to the Lodge to get his things ready while I wrestled with 300 pounds of flour, sugar, lard, sow-belly, etc. When everything was stashed away and the cabin looked neat again, I waited impatiently for Archie to come and see how nice it looked. I also wanted him to come and visit me. This was the first chance we had had to talk since he came to see me at home. The shindig at Forsythe didn't count, nor the silent trip in, and I'd been awake but a few hours since we arrived. He didn't come, and I decided to find out what was delaying him. Thinking it would take only a second to get to the lodge, I didn't put on my coat or the snowshoes. Out the door I went and sprawled face down in the snow. I got up, wiped my face, and peered about for Sunset Lodge. I could see only the slim stove-pipe sticking out like a periscope in a sea of snow.

Too mad and stubborn to return for my snowshoes, I waded hip deep in the snow and eventually reached the door. This was just a wooden frame a yard square, wrapped in heavy canvas. I gave this a lively rap, which made only a 'phuff, phuff, phuff'. No answer. In a temper I whacked it viciously, dislodging from the ridge-pole a huge hunk of snow, which plopped down on my head. Furious, frantic, and freezing, I tried to open the door. Inside Archie suddenly came to life. 'Who's there, who's there?' he sang out sweetly.

'It's me,' I shouted, heatedly. 'Who else?'

I heard him unfasten the latch, and fully expected him to be concerned and full of sympathy when he saw me standing there, shivering and covered with snow, but instead of helping me he chose to make a production of it, pretending that my calling was nothing less than a state visit. He swung the door open and, bowing grandly, invited me in.

'Madam, I am greatly honoured,' he gushed. 'So nice of you to come. Entrez, entrez.'

I got down on my hands and knees and crawled through the hole in the wall. Once in, I barely had standing room. Archie's place was in a turmoil. The already congested shack tent was now cluttered with a couple of gaping pack-sacks, the grub-box, etc., and a toboggan reaching from wall to wall was leaning against the table where Archie had been sanding it. I was dripping wet and waited for him to do something, but he was now feigning the embarrassed housewife caught with her apron down. He fluttered about – straightened his buckskin leggings, smoothed down his shirt, then, sticking out his tongue, pretended to lick his palms from wrist to finger-tip, and daintily patted his hair into place.

'Oh dear, oh dear,' he spluttered. 'I let the help go for the day, but don't worry. I'll manage. Tea shall be served anon.' Then he backed into the toboggan and fell flat on his back on the bunk, where he rolled with laughter, while I searched around for a nice dry towel. Referring to the incident much later, he told me, 'You looked so damned funny – a real greenhorn – I wanted to laugh so bad I could have died. That's why I put on

20

the act. And that fall was no accident – I needed an excuse to laugh. Yes sir, I just about died.'

After he finished sanding the toboggan, he put it and the snowshoes outside, buckled up the pack-sacks, and checked the grub-box. Soon the place was neat once more; in fact, with everything over at the other cabin, it was quite empty. Archie, satisfied that all was in readiness for tomorrow's journey, said, 'Well, let's get over there. I've got to make up a batch of bannock for the trip. I'll carry you over,' and smothering a laugh added, 'Or did you bring your snowshoes?' Of course he knew that I hadn't and to be caught without snowshoes in that country was as bad as being caught without your breeches.

We went outside, and Archie told me to get on his back. I refused. I had suffered enough indignities for one day, without adding insult to injury by riding piggy-back, but I allowed him to carry me in his arms.

'Say, kid,' he said, when we were at the door of Pony Hall, 'go and get your coat and put on your snowshoes. I want to show you where the water-hole is and how to look after it.'

'And just how does one look after a water-hole?' I enquired, sure that he was pulling my greenhorn leg again.

'I'm not kidding. There's more to it than is apparent.'

And so there is. If you are unfortunate enough to have a water-hole freeze over, it is easier to chip out a new one. Please don't take 'it is easier' and 'chip out' literally; as I elaborate you will understand why.

Before you start, you are faced with five feet of snow and at least four feet of ice. You begin by shovelling an area large enough to work in. After the shovel you initiate the axe, and when the axe handle gets too short for the job, you continue your labour with an ice chisel, an eight-foot pole with a steel chisel at the end. Since the blade on the steel chisel is only two inches wide, it takes time and perseverance to get down to the precious water.

On the way back to the cabin, Archie said, 'Remember when you are through with the water-hole to cover it up with at least a foot and a half of snow, and then stick the ice chisel nearby. That is your marker so you won't have any difficulty finding the water-hole at night or in a storm.'

When we reached the cabin, Archie said, 'Wait. Before we go in I want to show you the bear den.'

'A bear den?' I questioned, with mixed feelings.

'Sure, come on,' he said, leading the way into the bush. We came to a lean-to so covered with snow that it looked like an igloo. Terrified, I clung like a leech to Archie. We were nearly to the cave-like entrance when I held back. Archie said, 'Don't be scared – come on.' He struck a match and I peered with bulging eyes into the shadows, expecting to see a bear.

'I guess he hasn't come yet,' Archie said, as he reached in and brought out a roll of toilet tissue. 'I'm using this for bait.' This was the outhouse. He enjoyed his little joke immensely.

Back in the cabin Archie cooked supper and made bannock for his trip. I had never made bannock so I watched closely while he put the dough together. I couldn't help noticing his worried expression and asked him what was the matter. 'I'm worried', he said, 'about leaving you here alone. I didn't realize how little experience you've had in the bush. I guess after talking to your father I just took it for granted that you had more.'

'Oh yes,' I put in quickly. 'Papa did take me into the bush – a lot of times. We went berry picking together, and we used to camp out till we had enough to put up for the winter. And I went with him many times to make maple syrup and maple sugar. It was such fun. A real picnic.' I smiled happily at the recollection.

'Yeah, that's exactly what it was – a picnic,' Archie said dryly. 'But let me tell you, there's one hell of a difference between that and making the grade in the bush. It's a serious business, and I want you to listen carefully and do exactly as I say while I'm away. Except for the times that you've got to get in your wood and water, never leave the cabin. Always put on your snowshoes, even when going to the bear den. Don't fool around with the axe – there's enough wood to last a week out there. Keep a good supply of it in the cabin and see that you don't run out of kindling. And for God's sake be careful about fires – especially when you're handling the lamp. Of course, if this place burns down, you're lucky, because you can always go to Sunset Lodge. Generally, when a trapper's shack burns down he's out in the cold and that's it.'

After supper and a second batch of tea, Archie decided to go and get some sleep, for he intended to be on his way long before daylight. Before leaving he turned back at the door and said, 'I think it would be a good idea if I made a map so you'll be able to find your way out to Forsythe in case something happens and I can't get back.'

What does he mean, I wondered. Could he get lost or freeze to death, or be eaten alive? Such possibilities hadn't occurred to me before. Well, if I had nothing else to do while he was away, I could always worry.

The next morning I awoke to a very cold cabin. The fire was black out, but before re-lighting it I bounded outside in my pyjamas to see if there was smoke rising from the stove-pipe at Sunset Lodge. There wasn't, and I knew that Archie had gone. I stood rooted and took in my surroundings. I hadn't seen it by daylight before, and I marvelled at the sight. A fine, light snow shimmered down from above, and everything sparkled and glistened in the frosty air. It was beautiful! I was loath to break the spell, but the intense cold drove me back into the cabin and I had to crawl into bed to warm up before making a fire. I could hardly wait to go outside again.

After a hurried breakfast I spent the day outdoors, doing the chores and amusing myself in childish ways, such as printing our names on the lake, using my snowshoes to write in the snow. And when I opened the water-hole I lay down in the snow and looked into its black depths, imagining all sorts of mysterious happenings taking place down there.

The following day, against Archie's instructions, I tramped deep into the woods. How adventurous I felt. Caught in the spell of the north, I kept walking on and on, till it suddenly occurred to me that it was growing dark. I had no idea how many miles I'd travelled and nearly panicked. However, that extra shot of adrenalin got me home in less time than it takes to tell. The next day, just to show Archie that I wasn't entirely useless, even though I didn't cook bush-style, I decided to cut a pile of wood. Off I went in search of dead trees. I felled them, cut them into lengths convenient for carrying on snowshoes, and sawed and split the wood until it was dark. It was heavy work but I enjoyed every bit of it. It was fun playing house too. I sacrificed a pair of red and black bell-bottomed pyjamas to make some curtains for the window. These I thought looked very smart, and I kept the rug shining with a damp cloth and a comb.

I was busy polishing the enamel dishes and cutlery with wood ashes from the stove when suddenly out of the night came the hoot of an owl. It was loud and clear. It was about ten p.m. and the third day of Archie's absence. The owl hoot came again. It was uncommonly loud and quite near. It gave me the weirdest feeling. I couldn't stand the suspense any longer, so I went out to make sure that I'd heard what I thought I'd heard. Again it came, splitting the air. It came from down by the lakeshore. I jumped ten feet straight up and dashed back inside the cabin and pushed hard against the door. I was sure that anything capable of such a blast would have to be as big as a house. I was terrified. Clack, clack, rattle, crunch. Now it was at the door! I leaped like a lynx for the shotgun on the opposite wall. You can imagine my relief at the sound of Archie's voice asking, 'Hey in there – are you all right?'

I felt like an idiot. I had panicked, but I certainly wasn't going to let him know it. Quickly I replaced the gun in its rack and, striving for calmness, ran to the door. Poking my head out I stuttered, 'Yes, ye-es, I'm all right.'

'Say, you had me worried,' Archie replied. 'Were you asleep?'

'N-n-no . . . I mean yes.' At that time I didn't know that the call of the owl was Archie's way of announcing his coming and neither did I know that he could imitate this bird to perfection. At the drop of a hat he would come out with it with such intensity that it would bounce from here to there. So naturally, when I heard that racket at the door, I thought for sure that I was being invaded by a giant owl. What could be worse?

'I can't come in just yet,' he said. 'I've got to change clothes and start thawing out the joint. I'll be back though – make me something to eat, eh?'

I thought with horror of the bannock I'd made. It was heavy as lead and twice as solid. I'd like to think that it would have been passable had there been an oven in which to bake it, but the stove didn't have one so it had to be cooked on the top, like a pancake; but a bannock is two inches deep, and one must know to the split second when to flip it over or it will fall. The fire has to be just so, and that's where my ignorance came in. The fire was too high, and soon the bannock was burning. I flipped it over and 'plop' it went, face down in the pan, and that side started to smoke and burn. I had to open the cabin door to see what was going on. Anyway, the bannock was a total flop.

To offset the bannock deal, I thought it a good idea to try to look a little more appealing and immediately put the thought into action. I started slinging the make-up – vanishing cream, lipstick, and mascara (in those days you didn't put make-up on, you plastered it on), and changed into a low-cut blouse, and glamorous me was ready and waiting when Archie knocked. I was taken by surprise and delight when I opened the door and he strode in. He looked simply wonderful, I thought; the way he walked and the way he moved spoke volumes. Here in this harsh and isolated country he was at home. He radiated pride and confidence. He was clean-shaven and wore his hair brushed back in a seemingly careless fashion. He wore an ordinary work shirt, maroon in colour, dark-brown trousers, moccasin slippers, and the ever-present Hudson's Bay belt round his slim hips. Obviously the clothes did not make the man, at least in this case. Had the expression 'doll' existed at that time, I would have used it and, no doubt, as a consequence got my neck in a sling, for you can't call a man like Archie a doll.

But there he was, looking at me with his eyes like blue flames and his expression animated and cheerful. I had the unreal feeling that I was looking at a complete stranger – a tall and fascinating stranger – and I didn't quite know what to do. I was thinking that I'd made a big mistake in using this man as a substitute for my beloved Jesse James. Now I knew that I could no longer do that because a very real Archie Belaney had knocked my phantom lover for a loop the moment that he stepped in the door. To break my staring gaze he passed his hand before my eyes and said, 'Hey there, wake up. It's me – your old sidekick, remember?'

I came out of the long sleep and gushed, 'Boy oh boy, Archie, you look great tonight.'

Archie held up his hands as if to shield himself and said, 'Ah, ah, Reptile, you're flattering me again.' But he was pleased, I could see. The new curtains and other arrangements didn't go unnoticed, so I too was pleased. All through supper we indulged in light, nonsensical chatter. It was fun and I was glad to have him back. As for Archie, you'd think that he'd just returned from a vacation instead of a long, hard trip. He didn't seem tired in the least. When we finished eating, Archie left the table saying, 'I'd better go stoke 'er up. Got to keep a fire going. I have a few carcases over there to thaw out.'

I cleared the table while he was over at Sunset Lodge. The first thing he said when he returned was 'Say, do you know why I got you up here?' This was a peculiar question I thought, so I just said 'No.'

'Of course you don't. You're going to think I'm as crazy as a bedbug when I tell you this, but here it is. I sent you that telegram because I just couldn't wait to find out by mail whether you were all right or not.'

Puzzled, I asked him what he meant.

'Well,' he began, 'I did an awful stupid thing and as a consequence I just about kicked the bucket.'

'What? When? How?' I gasped in dismay.

'I accidentally got a dose of strychnine.'

As I was about to ask what business he had with poison, he shushed me by saying, 'Be quiet, Insect. I want to tell you something.' And he went on. 'The stuff raised hell with me – delirious and everything. Anyway, what got me worried was that some time during the course I saw you – as real as you are now. You were sitting on that bread box over there and looking at me so pitifully, as if you wanted me to come to you to help you; but struggle as I would, I couldn't. I tried to talk, but I couldn't do that either. Then you got up and went to the door. You turned and gave me a woebegone look as if you were sorry that I had let you down, then you went out and closed the door.

'I'm not superstitious, but that look haunted me. I just couldn't get it out of my mind, and I kept thinking all sorts of things that could be happening to you. I even thought that you might be dead. So as soon as I got back on my feet again, I made up my mind that I was going to ask you up, and started to build this cabin, though I had little hope that you would come. I was lucky because it was the slack trapping season and everything was at a standstill. I was able to get the help of a couple of trappers and we finished this cabin in no time flat. When I went out to Forsythe, your letter was there, the one saying that you weren't going to the convent after all. I gave out with a war whoop, because it meant one less obstacle I had to buck. But still I didn't know how you were, so I sent the wire right away, and here you are. Pretty smart, hey?'

'Yes, and I'm so glad you did. Except for that awful walk getting in here, I like this.'

Then, upon my insistence, he told me all about getting poisoned.

Most trappers use strychnine to get wolves and foxes, and I regret to say that this included Archie and me. It was a dreadful thing to do, I know, but trapping is cruel. Those lovely ladies clad in their exquisite furs would faint if they were to see the pain and torture suffered by only one of the many creatures whose lives must be taken to make up that fur coat or stole.

Archie began: 'I was camping out that night when, without thinking, I put the package of strychnine into the grub-box, of all places; but anything can happen, and does, when you're making camp and trying to get by when you're hungry and tired, or trying to keep from freezing to death. After I got back to Sunset Lodge from that trip, I did the usual chores, and when I was replenishing the grub-box for the next day's outing, I noticed this white powdery stuff spilled in the bottom of the box. Thinking it was sugar, I carefully scraped it up and poured it into the sugar dish. I've learned that when you are in the bush you save everything, even to a grain of sugar.

'The next morning I was in more than my usual rush. I had my breakfast over with before my tea was even cool enough to drink, so, with my pack-sack on my back, I waited, because I was going to have that tea if it killed me – and it damn near did. I didn't even get out of the door when all of a sudden I felt as if someone had hit me on the back of the head with a sack of flour. Then things started to jump and dance all over the shack. Immediately (and fortunately), I knew what had happened, so I grabbed for the dry mustard, dumped some into a cup of tea, and drank it down. Then I remembered that milk was an antidote for poisoning. I hauled out a precious tin of my milk from under the bunk and of course it was frozen solid. By this time I was getting stiff and felt as if I was walking backwards. I threw the can of milk into the stove to melt fast, and then I started to vomit. The mustard was doing its stuff. At the same time I managed to get the can of milk out of the stove before it exploded by raking it out of the coals, and I had some of that. I was as busy as the proverbial cat on a hot tin roof. At last I had to lie down, but between thawing out the milk from under the bunk and of course it was frozen solid. lie down for long at a time. I thought, "Sure as hell I've had it." '

'Oh Archie, you could have died,' I said.

'Yes, but as you see I didn't. In fact, I'm very much alive, but it's funny how the mind works at a time like that. I remember thinking how ridiculous it was to have gone through the trouble of being born; working and sweating, struggling to the last ditch, and taking oneself so damned seriously – the big shot – and then discovering that all it takes is a little pinch of white powder to blast you to hell.

'Then my Aunt Ada came to mind. Had she been there to see me lying in a trapper's little old shack with guts full of poison, she'd have said, "It serves you right. God knows I've done my duty by you – you've got your just desserts." '

'What makes you think that she would have said such a thing?' I wanted to know.

'Because I know my aunt.'

'Well, tell me about her.'

'Oh hell, it's not a pretty story. I'll try to make it short. I'm going to tell you this because you'll no doubt discover a few quirks in me that aren't exactly . . . ah . . . admirable.

'I was raised by my two aunts and a grandmother. We led a very secluded life. There weren't any playmates that I can remember – I suppose that's why I don't mind being alone. In fact, I prefer being alone to having a partner like most trappers do. I worshipped Aunt Carrie and my grandmother. Actually, they are the only pleasant memories I have of my childhood, and those are few, because each time I think that far back, thoughts of Aunt Ada come barging in and crowd everything else out.'

'From what you say, Aunt Ada must have been quite a woman. What was she like – was she beautiful?'

'Yes, she was a good-looking woman, always primped and starched, a perfectionist, a disciplinarian to the "nth" degree, and a snob. She went to finishing school and all that. She studied

German as well as the violin in Germany. All she lacked was a human heart.'

I urged him on, asking, 'Was she wicked? Come on, tell me everything.'

'Wicked isn't the word – but let it go. Instead of sending me off to school like any other kid, she decided that it would be better for me to stay at home and for her to teach me herself. She was a school-teacher and no doubt a good one; that is, you were going to learn if she had to pound it into you with a club. She was obsessed with the idea of turning me into some kind of genius, and the things that woman did to me shouldn't happen to man or beast. I could never get rid of her. She stuck to me like glue, she even supervised my dressing, as if I couldn't do a simple thing like that. Yet she fully expected me to tackle and do problems in arithmetic that would have stumped a kid four years older than I. The odd time that I did make the grade on a particularly difficult piece of work, I'd look up at her, kind of expecting a word of approval, or a little pat on the back, but all I ever got from her was "Well, so you ought." I'm a southpaw, and the punishment I went through on that account you'd never believe. She'd whack my hand with that pointer of hers, and many were the times that, if by accident I happened to touch a pen or pencil with my left hand, she pulled me off the chair by the hair. Then there were the music lessons and the Bible study. You'd imagine that those subjects would touch the heart of almost anyone and bring out the best in them, but that was a laugh. She was every bit as much the brute in that as she was in everything else.

'Getting me dressed to go out was another ordeal. She'd make me put on several different outfits, suits and such, and this would go on until something suited her mood for that particular day. You'd think that once I was dressed that would be the end of it; but no, then she'd start pulling, twisting, straightening, and prodding at my clothes till I wanted to scream. To this day I can't trust myself to be fitted for a suit because I know damn well that before the tailor was through it would be either him or me on that floor, out cold – colder than a mackerel.

'What an intensely frustrated woman she must have been. She was never married, and being loveless and childless for so many years it was only natural for her to slough off all those bottled-up emotions at the first chance she had, and that chance came when I arrived on the scene. I was her safety valve. If I hadn't been around she would have exploded herself right into the mad house. I suppose in her way she loved me, or she wouldn't have given so much of herself towards my upbringing. I can just imagine her thinking, "By gad, I'll make a gentleman out of him if it kills him" (and, by gad, she damn near did).

'Speaking of men, gentle or otherwise, I hadn't a chance in those days to talk to one. There was never any around – an abnormal situation for a boy. I suppose that was another reason Aunt Ada had me cowed. She had me scared to death for a while. I thought of suicide quite a few times. Once I tried to smother myself with a pillow – a nice soft way to go – but joking aside, she came close to making a lily-livered coward out of me. She'd have liked that – me as putty in her hands – to break my spirit. Luckily I put up a fight, and she succeeded only in making a devil out of me. Then came the time when I dared to hate her. I was surprised that she didn't suspect this, because I'd been under the impression that she knew my innermost thoughts, and finding out otherwise, I enjoyed wallowing in my hate for her – glad that I was putting something over at last. But that stage didn't last long because I soon found myself planning ways to kill her.'

'You didn't kill her?' I asked, with a satanic wish that he had, because I had an aunt that I thought deserved the same fate.

Archie said, 'I had laid my plans; my decision was made to do her in and put an end to my misery. No kidding, I was dead serious in this. My choice of weapons was a bust of Bach or Brahms – I forget which. I can't remember either whether it was sculpted in clay or cast in bronze. Anyhow, I figured it would be heavy enough to serve my purpose. This thing stood between two huge potted plants at the entrance of an alcove. It was an ideal place to hide, and my aunt always went there to read the paper. She was one of those people who did the same things at the same time every day. She never varied a second. Why, you could set your watch by her, so it wasn't hard to anticipate where she would be at a certain time.

'The idea was to push the statue over and crush her as she passed, and that's exactly what I did.'

He hesitated, and went on, 'Well sir, I saw her coming that evening, and I waited till she got to the exact spot and I gave that thing a push. I gave it all I had. The jolt separated the bust of old Bach from his pedestal and he crashed down on my head and knocked me out cold.

'Now I look back with amusement at this little boy trying to slay his dragon, but just the same she was an ogress if there ever was one. It wasn't the physical abuse that she dealt out that used to hurt so much, it was the mental torture that she inflicted. She was an artist at that, and I hated her guts.

'When I first came to live in the bush and I got to thinking of her, I'd get so mad I'd take my rifle out and fire round after round into the ground, hoping that one of my bullets would find her in hell; then I would swear and curse like a maniac till I was exhausted – I'm not exaggerating. I used to get a kick out of doing what I knew would have horrified her. But sometimes I got carried away and did things that even I felt were wrong, and that gave me a lot more satisfaction. Those were the times that I didn't have to deliberately go against whatever teachings she had driven into me. It was my own doing that got me into trouble, and it felt good knowing that she hadn't gobbled me up to the extent that I was just another Aunt Ada going around in long pants.'

I thought this very funny – but not Archie. He immediately got up and said, 'I'd better get over to my shack and make another fire. I suppose the darned thing has gone out again. Say, it's just occurred to me that I've been doing all the talking, so now I want to hear all about you. Let's make a night of it.'

'But,' I objected, 'it is awful late.'

'It's never late till morning and then it's early.'

I sat silently, wondering what I could say about myself that could possibly be of interest to him. However, his first question got the ball rolling. 'Your father told me that you were Iroquois. Is that right?'

This was a quick switch, for I hadn't discussed my ancestors with anyone since my grandmother and I were together. I finally answered, 'That's right. We are Mohawks.'

'But your father said you were Iroquois.'

'Yes, I know, he always says that, but Grandma told me that we were just one of a band of Indians that made up the confederacy of the Five Nations, called the Iroquois. . . .'

Archie interrupted me. 'Hold it, hold it. Let's get this straight. Do you mean to say that the Iroquois are the Five Nations, that they are not a distinctive band or tribe?'

'That's right,' I answered, and went on to explain. 'The Iroquois are the Mohawks, Oneidas, Onondagas, Cayugas, Senecas, and Tuscaroras. They – the Tuscaroras – were the last to join us, and then we became the Six Nations.'

Archie exclaimed, 'Well, how about that? Though I've read a lot on Indians, I didn't know that.'

'I find most people don't. I guess they're just not interested,' I said, 'but I remember my grandmother having some awful arguments with friends. Most of her friends were French and insisted that the Hurons were of the Confederacy when, actually, they were hereditary enemies of ours. They even fought beside the French, whereas we were with the English. That is, until our leaders realized that their country was slipping away from them under the guise of treaties and reservations. That was when a little group of patriots – or rebels if you wish – chose to take to the woods, and from there start a war on their own. Determined to regain their lands, they began to strike with raids and attacks on the settlements, both French and English, killing everyone – women in particular, because they were the producers of their kind – and it became the rule to take no prisoners, in case they escaped and revealed the Indians' location and what they were up to. They used the hit-and-run method. Many of their more daring escapades were when they had to go for guns and ammunition. My great-grandmother, Mary Robinson, was captured on one of these forays.'

'But' said Archie 'you just told me that the taking of prisoners was no longer allowed – or was she taken in some other war?'

I didn't know offhand, but I thought that I'd give him some sort of answer, so I said, 'I'm not sure, but I think it was just a massacre.'

'Just a massacre,' Archie exclaimed as he held the tea-pail over my cup. 'Would you care for another cup of blood? Oh, pardon me, I mean tea?' He poured out tea and became serious again, asking, 'In what year was your ancestor taken?'

'It happened two years before my grandmother was born, so it must have been 1810.'

Archie waited for me to go on, but thinking the subject closed I said no more.

He prodded me impatiently. 'What's the matter? Can't you remember any more?'

'Can't remember what?' I questioned.

'Oh for Christ's sake, what happened to Mary Robinson? In what part of Canada did this take place? Did it happen in the War of 1812?'

Although these stories had been told and retold to me by my grandmother – she was a century-old woman – I was but a child at the time and my childhood memory could only relate a certain amount of the happenings of those days, especially on the spur of the moment. I found these questions of Archie's too cold and concise to answer without first unravelling the story as it came to me. And another thing that didn't help was the way Archie was gulping down cup after cup of tea, and throwing me penetrating glances and saying 'Well, well,' at every gulp.

In 1810 or thereabouts, the leader of a band of revolutionaries was Naharrenou, hereditary chief of the Mohawks. (Although he was my great-great-grandfather, I am unable to spell his name, but it is pronounced as above.) Actually the name Anahareo, the name Archie calls me in his writings, is taken from Naharrenou.

This chief made it known among his people that he was going to leave before the invaders made a slave of him, as they had done with those they had conquered in the past. It was an honour among the Mohawks to be selected for torture at the stake, for this meant that the visitors thought him the bravest of the brave. It was like being presented with a medal of valour. Of the two evils, slavery and torture, the Mohawks preferred torture to the ignominy of becoming a slave. When Naharrenou realized that the British, their former allies, were strong enough in the land to lay down laws to the Indians, he asked those who thought as he did to go into the wilderness and fight from there until the best man won. Naharrenou took his leave of the Lake of Two Mountains, south-west of Montreal, with a group of about three hundred, including women and children (unless they wanted to be parted forever from their menfolk, the women had to go along). From hidden and strategic points they struck at the white settlements time and time again and moved camp when advisable. I have no idea how long they'd been at this when Naharrenou received a gunshot wound and was confined to the camp, and the leadership fell to Kanistonou, his son – my great-grandfather.

It was on one of his own raids that Kanistonou met his match. A young woman fled the village at the first onslaught of this particular attack and ran deep into the woods until she fell from exhaustion. It was there, on the following day, that Kanistonou found her. He found himself unable to kill her, and he couldn't send her back to her settlement, for all there were dead. There was the strict rule against taking prisoners, and since he couldn't bring himself to kill her, he sent the girl back with one of his men, with orders that she was not to be harmed in any way before his return.

And so it was that Mary Robinson was treated by the Mohawk people as becomes the charge of a war chief. But, on the other hand, the war chief himself on his return ran into a barrage of criticism that would have floored a less obdurate man. Of course they'd awaited his return with impatience because it was up to him to finish the job. But he refused to kill the prisoner. When he announced that he would marry her instead, the council emphatically stated that this was out of the question. For one thing, it would set a bad example. It was finally agreed that Mary Robinson could remain among them, with the stipulation that Kanistonou, or anyone else, would refrain from touching the prisoner in any way. So, for two years, Mary lived with the Mohawks, learning how to cope with her new way of life. She became expert in everything she put her mind to, and when she and Kanistonou expressed the wish to be married, no one objected. Their first child, my grandmother, was born in 1812 or thereabouts.

The War of 1812 proved more of a benefit than a disaster to the band of isolated rebels, because they took advantage of the confusion of war, or a battle, when no one suspected that they had an enemy in their midst. They were past masters by now at striking, and fading into the shadows with guns and loot. However, this was to prove their downfall, for after the war was over they became more daring, either out of necessity or from over-confidence. Their presence became known, and the soldiers went in and killed them all, except for a few women and children.* Mary Robinson, Kanistonou, and a new-born son were killed, and Grandmother, scarcely more than a babe-in-arms, was taken to Montreal and given to the nuns. She received her education in a convent there, and then, as a young lady, went to join her people at Oka, the Lake of Two Mountains.

On her arrival there, Grandma presented a parchment scroll to the chief of the Mohawks. This was a missive that Mary Robinson had written for Naharrenou when the band of rebels saw the writing on the wall and knew their fight was about over. Kanistonou and Naharrenou had urged Mary Robinson to return to her own people before it was too late. On her adamant refusal to leave, Naharrenou had asked her to write a letter to a relative of his in Oka, who had preferred to stay there under foreign laws and restrictions rather than join the fight for freedom. Mary agreed, so, on parchment and in his own blood, she wrote Naharrenou's farewell. In his letter he also asked his relative to take care of his two grandchildren, if they lived. The relative was to recognize them as his by Naharrenou's mark. (I don't know what this mark was.)

If it hadn't been for this missive and Mary's sketchy account on the same parchment of her five years among the Mohawks, along with the account given by the few women who had survived the soldiers' attack, Grandma wouldn't have known who she was.

I imagine it was because of the important looking document that was attached to Grandma's wrist, and the fact that she was part white, that she was taken to the convent instead of to Oka, where the rest of the refugees were taken. Grandma said, 'Pretty soon many people came and claimed they were my relations and I was happy because I had thought all along that I was part of the convent and wasn't born like everybody else. Many other

* To our knowledge, no written records confirm or deny this account, which seems to contradict the general assumption that peace prevailed between the Iroquois and the British Canadians in Upper Canada after 1784. It is possible that the account refers to troubles in New York State or New England. It is included here in deference to the customary accuracy of Iroquois' oral tradition. (Editor)

people came and touched me and tried to feel like they were touching one of their own who had gone with Naharrenou.'

Grandmother married in Oka and soon afterward she and her husband secretly stole away from the oppression and poverty there. They took almost the same trail as had Naharrenou – they too had to travel off the beaten trail – and this led them to where Belleville is now, or just north of it. There they remained for twenty-five years and raised a family of eleven. Then, owing to the fact that Indians were unable to own property at that time, they were forced to move off the land that they had cleared and called home, because it was taken from them by those who were fortunate enough to be able to own land.

They decided to travel in a north-westerly direction until they came to an acceptable spot that would be far enough away so they wouldn't need to move again for a few years. There were no roads, and it was a long trek from Belleville to the Ottawa River, where they settled. They had a plough and other farm implements, ten horses, and twenty-one head of cattle when they arrived at Mattawa, and that is where my Grandmother died in 1920 at the age of 108. Our family never lived on any Indian reserves.

I was born at Mattawa on June 18, 1906. When I was about four years old, my mother died. Though I didn't know what was actually happening, I do remember the day she died because my aunts, uncles, two grandmothers and Papa were kneeling in prayer by her bed. When finally my father came out of the bedroom, he looked very different – like some stranger. He walked right by me without seeing and went out of the house and down to the lake, alone.

Later, I remember my father, looking pale and sorrowful, leading me to his mother, placing my hand in hers, and saying in Mohawk, 'Mother, I am asking you to take care of this little one.' Grandmother was ninety-five when we started out on our new life together. (After Mother's death my year-old brother was taken by my maternal grandmother; a sister, Johanna, age nine, and a brother, Edward, age seven, went to live with Aunt Kate in North Bay, Ontario.)

I've been told that my grandmother seemed to come alive as soon as she thought that she was needed again. I believe this, because otherwise a person of her years couldn't have done all she did for me. Of course, we had a woman in to do our housework, Grandma being too old, and I too young, to do it ourselves. For all that, Grandma was not idle, nor was I, for, with amazing patience, she taught me to sew, bead, make deerskin mitts and moccasins, embroider, crochet, knit, tan hides, and make soap. She taught me, too, the lore of medicinal herbs: the golden leaf for cramps; steambaths, using the liquid from boiled cedar boughs and red cherry bark. This was good for anything and everything. Then there was the root of a thousand roots. This, too, was supposed to cure everything. All that she taught me has been of great value to me through the years. Even now, there is seldom a day goes by that I don't think of her. I suppose it's because in everyday life there are always happenings, problems, crises that remind me of her and of the way she would have handled any situation. In fact, Archie tired of my always telling him how Grandma would have done this or that. I was most fortunate in having her raise me – what a devil I'd have been without her.

We went to church together, where she sang in the choir, and at one time had played the organ but was now too stiff with age to do so. I remember her beautiful soprano and how, at last, it let her down. How I cried. It was an unnecessary grief, for when her friends came (they were all over eighty) they always had a singsong, Grandma at the organ and I on a low bench doing the pumping. There were more bad notes and laughter than music.

Most of all I loved her huge trunk, full of souvenirs and momentos, each one telling a story of romance, tragedy, or adventure. Grandma's eyes would light up with the telling of some stories and smoulder with the telling of others.

Then there was her book. Grandma had learned to speak her own language only after she left the convent, but she'd always yearned to translate prayers, history, and little anecdotes, etc., from the French into Mohawk. She was a middle-aged woman before she was able to accomplish this. It was an immense book, all written in her fine hand with a quill. Along the margins she had painted vines, leaves, and birds, and between chapters, beautiful little flowers.

Our bedroom walls were covered with things. There were pictures of Louis XV, Marie Antoinette, Queen Anne, Victoria, and Napoleon, whom she loved, and later, Kitchener and Foch. These are only a few. The shelves were laden with statuettes of different saints.

She loved reading and gardening. I guess she must have been a forerunner of Burbank, the way she tended her fruit trees, apple, cherry, and plum. She had an orange tree, which, with her pampering, grew to four feet in height, unusual in our climate. She also experimented with watermelons, musk-melons, and sweet potatoes, and her flower gardens were marvellous. To this day I always associate lilacs with Grandma.

To while away our winter evenings we'd pop our own garden corn, or roast apples on top of the stove, where they spluttered noisily and rolled about as if alive. They were delicious. Another delicacy that Grandmother devised was to split a turnip in two and then scrape out the juicy meat with a knife, all the time telling more of her stories. But all good things must come to an end, and so did this.

The rains came in the form of an aunt and uncle with four very spoiled and pampered children. They came to take care of Grandmother and me. It isn't sporting to speak ill of the dead, so I will endeavour to be kind.

My aunt was the exact opposite of Archie's Aunt Ada. Miss Belaney's approach left much to be desired, but her efforts were to Archie's advantage, whereas my aunt simply relegated me to the role of nothing more than a drudge and servant to her children. I had to jump – and I mean jump – at their every wish. She didn't bother to teach me anything, spiritual or otherwise. It was just 'Do this, do that'. And she wasn't what you'd call energetic herself, because she would keep me home from school on wash-days, scrub-days, shopping-days and so on, until I was so far behind in my class that I began to cheat by paying a girl a couple of grades above mine to do my arithmetic for me.

The whole thing sickened me and I began to play hooky. My chances of getting an education were going to pot, but Aunty couldn't have cared less. There were no report cards in those days, so she really didn't know what I was doing.

Off I'd go on those summer mornings, happy as a lark, to a day of hooky and adventure in the woods, or to a lake, or a

Anahareo posed casually in deerskin dress, probably in the early 1930's.

EDITOR'S NOTE

The pictures have been chosen, from many available, to
show as broad a range as possible of the author's life with
Grey Owl. Unfortunately, many photographs carried
little in the way of caption material, and it has often been
impossible to confirm dates and places.

Before he assumed the name Grey Owl, Archie Belaney looked his future role. Left is Billy Miller, and right is Jim Espaniol.

Grey Owl with beaver at Riding Mountain National Park in 1931. The beaver is probably one of Jelly Roll's May kittens.

Grey Owl feeds young twin moose from a bottle, Riding Mountain National Park.

Grey Owl returns by canoe to his cabin at Prince Albert National Park, probably in summer, 1932.

Jelly Roll builds her channel entrance to the cabin at Prince Albert National Park.

Probably on tour in the 1930's, Grey Owl combined the dress of white man and Indian.

Aged about thirteen years, Archie Belaney posed with his dog in England.

pasture full of horses. Or, I could get a boat – several in fact – that is, if I wasn't caught taking them. The same applied to horses. What with climbing trees, picking berries, cherries, and sweet plums when they were in season, and swimming, fishing, boating or canoeing, and horseback riding, it was a ball.

While exploring one afternoon I discovered an old shanty built by the river drivers many years before. It had a birch-bark roof (layers of birch bark weighed down with rocks and earth), an ideal place when it rained. I soon had the shanty in fine shape and well supplied with all the necessities of life. I had a feather tick and blankets; a cooking pot, fry-pan, and dishes, fishing-tackle, and food which I had bought with my own pocket-money. With the fish I caught, and vegetables from the handiest garden, I was having the time of my life. I have my aunt to thank for my getting away with this for as long as I did. She was so involved with her own family she couldn't see any further than her own children – let alone this wandering little crook.

My father was home only every second week and was not aware of what was going on until I told him, but this was only after the weather got too cold for me to stay in the shanty. He became so angry – not with me, but with Aunt Bessie – that he went up to Uncle Frank and told him a thing or two about his wife, and they would have come to blows if Grandma hadn't come out and struck them both with a little switch and told them to stop at once. Although Papa never, never gave me a licking, I was quite prepared for one when I told him about the hooky deal, but all he did was to get us a house, and then he sent for my brother Ed, fifteen, and my sister Jo, seventeen, who had been with Papa's sister in North Bay. Aunt Kathy had no children of her own, and her husband, a locomotive engineer, was away much of the time, so naturally she enjoyed having them, and they, unlike me, went to school.

We moved into our house and were together again for the first time since Mother's death. Ed and Jo were practically strangers to me when they first came, for we'd had only yearly visits up to then. It wasn't too long, however, before our home was happy and gay. Papa took a contract to build a house for his friend Charlie Chenier and was able to be home with us every night. Jo and Ed were still attending school, but I refused to return, mortified at the thought of being a 'giant' among my classmates. Father let me have my way.

I said that I had a ball playing hooky, but this isn't true. I had been too long with Grandma, a religious, strait-laced woman, for my conscience to be quieted so easily, and each time it pointed an accusing finger at me I'd look for something worse to do, hoping that it would go away. I started swimming with the boys down at the sand bar. This, in those days, was nothing less than a crime. I could swim like a fish, and my being a girl was a novelty. I was accepted by them. At first I was secretive about joining the boys in swimming, but later I became less sensitive on that score and even introduced lacrosse to the gang, as we had the only set of lacrosse sticks in town. The game became more popular than baseball, and I was always 'in' when it came to hockey, so I certainly wasn't popular with the girls around there. In fact, they would rather have died than be caught talking to me. Anyway, I always thought of their games as being watered down and in slow motion.

Finally the boys became girl-conscious. Of course, they'd never think of dating me; after all, I was just one of them – and, curiously, I didn't think this odd. Eventually, the gang petered out, and I found myself alone again. I began my solitary wanderings, as I had done before.

Archie was as good a listener as he was a talker, and the time went quickly. The tea-pail, coal oil, and wood-pile took a beating that night, for we stayed up till daylight. In that part of the country day came at about eight a.m. at that time of year.

We were two people in the snow-bound wilderness of the far north, really strangers to each other and with backgrounds poles apart. Archie's grandfather was a poet. He had received recognition from the Queen of England while my own great-grandfather was in the wilds of North America, literally still on the war-path.

It was almost time for me to leave for home, but before Archie could take me 'out', he had to go over a line of traps that he hadn't tended for weeks. It would be an overnight trip.

I wanted to go with him and said, 'Oh, that will be fun. Can I go?'

'That, my dear friend and neighbour, is impossible,' he said, as if that ended that.

'But why?' I asked, feeling a wave of stubbornness sweep over me.

'Because it's going to be a rough trip, and besides that we'd have to sleep out.'

I won him over, finally, and early the next morning – so early that it was still pitch-dark out – we headed into a snow storm, not a fluttering of wafting snow, but a fierce, driving wind that whipped the snow, sending it in all directions, cutting the face and stinging the eyes as we walked across the frozen lake. I wondered why he didn't turn back. I certainly wasn't going to suggest it, not after the great howl I had put up about coming along.

This was marten, fisher, and lynx country, so all the traps were set deep in the bush where the wind couldn't get in too much of its dirty work. No doubt Archie had this in mind when he continued the journey in spite of the storm.

We'd gone about four miles when we came across some moose tracks – a trench really – because the snow was so deep the moose had to plow through, leaving quite a furrow. Immediately Archie was the hunter. He stretched to his full height with his nose up as if sniffing the air – and I guess he was. He got down into the trench to find out whether the moose was a bull or a cow, and also to see which direction it was travelling. He stood up and said, 'It's a bull, and I'm going to get him.' (The way to tell whether it is a bull or a cow is by feeling the hard-packed snow made by the hoof. If it's rounded, it's a cow.)

In a businesslike manner, Archie turned the loaded toboggan on its side to prevent the bottom from icing, unlashed the rifle from the load, and away we went. There is a great deal to stalking a moose. Archie has described the 'still hunt' to perfection in his *The Men of the Last Frontier*.

Eventually, we sighted the buck. Archie raised his rifle and fired, and that was that. The animal was dead when we came up to it. Archie tramped the snow, packing it to make a place to work. After he had skinned the moose, he slit it up the belly and removed the innards. As the warmth of the intestines hit the cold air, it created a great cloud of steam. It wasn't a pretty picture. Archie cut up the meat, wrapped it in the hide, and covered it with snow, and off we went again. I wished that I had stayed home.

Some miles later, Archie stopped, unhitched himself from the toboggan line, and said, 'It's time to eat.' Before he finished saying this he was away into the bush to get wood for a fire. Always in a hurry! In that country of deep snow it takes quite a time to make a fire, because you must make a platform of green logs on which to build it. Without a platform, the fire would melt itself out of sight before the tea was half made.

I was flabbergasted, to say the least, at the victuals Archie offered me for lunch. They consisted of frozen bannock, lard, and fried sow-belly.

It was early afternoon, and, on the trail again, Archie turned and in a hushed voice said, 'There's something in this one.' As he said this, there was a swift movement in the direction he pointed, and then I saw a little brown animal. It was about twenty-five feet ahead of us.

'Here's your marten,' Archie said, and to my horror I saw the poor little creature pulling as far as the chain of the trap would allow, trying to escape. Its forearm was bloodied where the jaws of the trap had snapped shut.

'Get him out of there quick!' I shouted. 'How are we going to get him out of that trap without hurting him?'

The marten tossed and jumped, trying to get away. I wrenched off my coat and was going to throw it over the animal to keep it from biting us while we released it from the trap.

Archie held his trail axe in his hand, and with the handle he pointed down the trail, saying, 'You're not going to like this. I advise you to go over there for awhile.'

'What are you talking about? Let's get him out of there.'

Archie, his expression like a rock, said 'I'm sorry.' Then he bent towards the terrified animal and, with three swift strokes, using the handle of the axe as a club, he hit the marten across the head. It lay there in the snow, jerking in quick little spasms, its nose bleeding; and then, mercifully, it died. I was so angry with Archie that if I hadn't got sick I believe I would have done the same thing to him. He knew how I felt, but didn't say anything. What was there to say?

The marten is a very pretty animal, like a miniature fox, but prettier, I think, because of its daintiness and the deep orange markings about the throat and chest. This was the first one I'd ever seen.

For the rest of the day I could hardly put one snowshoe before the other. I felt as if I were carrying a ton. First the moose, now the marten. I was depressed, angry, and disgusted. Before the afternoon was over Archie picked up another marten and two lynx, but, thank goodness, they were dead when we came to them.

At the end of the day's tramp we came to a heavily wooded bay, and there Archie said brightly, 'Here's a good spot to spend the night.' I received this news with gladness and looked sharply around for the refuge that was to harbour us for the night, but all I could see was a world of snow and trees, so I said, 'I can't see it.'

'Can't see what?' Archie asked, as he took the big axe from the load.

'Where we're supposed to stay tonight,' I answered in a wee small voice, because I was beginning to have some suspicions. He had said that we would sleep out, but I hadn't thought that he'd meant it literally. I thought he'd only meant that we would spend the night away from Pony Hall – well, it just never dawned! But here he was, digging with his snowshoe, making some kind of hole. Surely he doesn't expect me to sleep in that, I thought.

Archie said, 'You'd be a lot better off if you got in here and did some digging too. It'll keep you warm till we get a fire going.'

Feeling that I was digging my own grave, I did as he said. I eventually got up enough courage to ask, 'What are we supposed to be doing?' Archie threw me a long, wondering look. 'We're getting the camp up,' he answered, and went back to his shovelling.

'The camp is down – there?' I exclaimed, aghast.

This ridiculous presumption brought forth gales of laughter.

43

Then he asked me to pack the snow as he shovelled it out. I got down on my knees and began patting the snow with my mittened hands.

'No, not that way! Stamp it down with your snowshoes,' said Archie, somewhat hopelessly.

What we were actually doing was excavating a pit large enough for two beds, the grub-box, and an eight-foot fire. This excavation was the depth of the snow, normally seven feet. Even after packing it down, the snowbank that encircled us was six feet high. This served as an efficient wind-break.

What with the toboggan sheet (a tarpaulin) overhead as a shelter, and a carpet of boughs, I was surprised at how comfortable a sleeping-out camp could be. It takes a seasoned woodsman to know how to lean his lean-to.

After supper, sitting in the warmth of the fire and watching the flaming logs tint our walls of snow to pink and gold, I listened to Archie talk. Those who have heard Grey Owl lecture will understand that it is impossible for me to recount what he said then, or how he expressed it – particularly when he spoke of the wilderness and everything connected with it.

As Archie talked, a group of snowshoe rabbits, attracted by the light of the fire, appeared atop the snowbank, and there they were, sitting in a row as if they too were listening.

We returned to Pony Hall the evening before Archie was to take me to Forsythe and to the train that would take me home. Archie made a valiant effort to be bright and gay, but finally ceased trying, and I too remained silent as I collected my things and began to pack. I was unhappy at the thought of leaving 'my little cabin in the woods', and sorry, too, to be leaving Archie. It seemed but yesterday that I had come. Archie sat by the table smoking his pipe. Whatever he was thinking he did not share with me.

At last he got up, filled the stove with wood, and put water on for tea. Then he moved a seat over to the window. 'C'mon,' he said, 'let's put out the light and look through the window.'

'Now what would we do a crazy thing like that for?'

'Oh, c'mon. I can show you all kinds of things out there in the trees, in the shadows, in the snow.'

Thinking it an odd request, I nevertheless joined him, and there we sat silently in the gloomy darkness. I soon tired of that game and wished he would say something, but he wasn't in a talkative mood. However, after much coaxing, he told me of his first experience in the Canadian woods.

/\\\.\\.\\.\\.\\.\\.\\

In 1906 he had arrived in Toronto, where he worked as a clerk in a men's-wear shop. Hating every minute of it, he couldn't wait until he had enough money to take him to Cobalt, where there had been a recent discovery of silver. (Cobalt, Ontario, 330 miles north of Toronto, was then one of the richest silver districts in the world.)

Archie quit his job and joined the hordes of claim-stakers. Not having the necessary cash, he had to get off the train 130 miles short of his destination and walk the rest of the way.

After a day's tramp over the railroad ties, his city shoes were in shreds. He had no food with him and, worse still, it was early spring and the frost was still in the ground. He hadn't even an axe, a necessary thing for one who has to sleep in the open without a bed-roll. The first night he made a fire of twigs, which soon burnt itself out, but being tired, he slept on regardless. The second night was the same, except that he was hungrier and his feet were blistered. The third day found him definitely ill, but he staggered on till he came to a river. Thirsty from fever, he stumbled down to the icy water and drank greedily, and there, on the riverbank, he fell asleep. Fortunately, just before dark, Bill, a trapper, happened by in a canoe, and he sighted Archie lying on shore and went to investigate. He found that he had a mighty sick boy on his hands.

Bill made a sort of bed in the bottom of his canoe and somehow got Archie in. After paddling day and night he at last pulled ashore at Timagami, a village in northern Ontario.

There wasn't a doctor within miles, but there was an Indian medicine man in the village. Old Ag-Nu, as he was called, knew his herbs well, but he still resorted to his weird chantings, his drum, and his bag of charms. Ag-Nu lived alone in an old log shack, its walls blackened by smoke and age. Its furnishings were home-made, except for the old stove, which was legless and sat in the middle of the dirt floor. Bill managed to get

Archie into the Ojibway medicine man's shack and onto a bunk.

Archie, during a conscious moment, saw the old man reach up for something that was clinging to the wall. It was yellowish-white and came alive when touched, its many tentacles waving in the air, grasping, reaching. The old man put it on a flat rock and began pounding it slowly and methodically with a wooden hammer. 'He's killing it,' Archie thought.

This 'thing' was the herb 'the root of a thousand roots' and it would dull the pain in the lungs. Archie drank this and went to sleep, only to awaken at intervals. Once he awoke to see Ag-Nu arranging rocks around a huge black pot on the red-hot stove. Then the old man went to a dark corner and returned with a bundle. He put this down on the mat of cedar boughs and opened it, revealing various necklaces of animal claws, bones, and loops of fur, a headpiece, a medicine bag, and a drum. He removed his shirt, placed a necklace around his neck, attached something to his left wrist, and donned his conjuror's headdress. Holding the medicine bag over the steaming brew of cedar and cherry bark, he began to sing, and dash the hot rocks with the medicine, causing a great cloud to rise and fill the room with steam. He repeated this procedure again and again. At intervals he beat on the drum and chanted, imploring the Great Spirit to lay his healing hand upon his patient.

Ag-Nu, rivulets of sweat dripping from him, conjured on and on into the night. Suddenly, he ended, rose, and went to the bunk. He stood motionless as a statue, peering down at Archie. Archie gazed weakly up at the Indian standing there naked to the waist, his bronze skin glistening in the lamp light. Archie moved his lips, but couldn't speak, couldn't think for the beating, pounding noise reverberating from every wall. He wished it would stop – it made him dizzy. He closed his eyes, but opened them again to see where the noise originated. Then he saw it – a drum suspended in mid-air, held there by no visible means. The drumsticks, manipulated by some unseen hand, pounded on the drum, which now pulsed with a life of its own.

The more he tried to comprehend this strange phenomenon, the more confused and fearful he became. Now the drum came closer. He wanted to cry out, but at that moment Ag-Nu, with a cup in his hand, appeared at his bedside. The old man raised the damp head of his patient and gently put the cup to his lips, once more giving Archie the medicine from the root of a thousand roots. The next day he had passed the crisis and when he opened his eyes he was startled to find himself in this old shack with the blackened walls. He hadn't dreamed this up in delirium after all.

It was quiet in the cabin; there wasn't a sound. Archie remembered the old man and glanced about the room, but could see no one. Then he noticed a heap of blankets on the floor. With difficulty he raised himself for a closer look. As he suspected, Ag-Nu was lying there asleep. He lay on his pillow, thinking, wondering, and greatly distraught. He had no idea where he was or how he had got there. He did know that he was terribly weak, without money, and in a strange place. Filled with misgivings, for what seemed hours he lay and wondered what had happened to the romance and the exciting adventure he was seeking. His mood of despondency was interrupted by someone at the door. Archie thought at last he would know where he was and looked expectantly at the door. He saw an Indian girl, tall and slender, coming towards him with a bowl in her hand. She was wearing a long, full skirt, a bright, flowered blouse, and a colourful kerchief draped loosely about her shoulders. She had a heart-shaped face, high cheek bones, and black eyes filled with mirth and mischief. Smiling, she approached Archie and offered him the bowl.

'You drink,' she said.

Archie saw that the bowl contained some kind of broth.

'What is it?' he asked.

'Is boiled fish heads – is good, you drink,' she urged.

Archie thanked her and, shuddering inwardly, tipped the bowl; to his surprise he found it pleasant.

Pleased that he liked it, the girl said, 'I get some more.'

Archie grasped her arm as she reached for the dish, saying, 'No, please don't go. I want to ask you something.'

The girl tilted her head questioningly.

Archie went on. 'What is your name?'

'Angele,' she answered.

'Angele . . . in English it means angel. It's a lovely name, so be an angel, and tell me where I am.'

She thought this very funny and began to giggle, unable to answer for laughing.

'Where am I? What is the name of this place?' Archie asked with some annoyance.

She found this even funnier, but Archie's expression reached the mark, and she choked back her laughter and said, 'This is Timagami,' and this was the extent of her elaboration. To her, Timagami was the hub of the earth, and she thought that the mere mention of the name would be explanation enough. From his blank look she knew Archie had never heard of the place, and, disgusted, she said, 'I guess you don't know nutting. I go now.'

'No, wait a minute!'

'I gotta go sew my dress. I go dance tonight.'

Frivolity of any description being furthest from his mind, Archie repeated 'Dance?'

She threw him a withering look, as if to say, 'The poor fellow, he doesn't even know that.' 'Of course, there's a dance tonight. There's one every night.' Waiting for no more questions, she left.

With so much fun and things to do in the village, Angele had little time for the sick. Archie saw her only on the occasions when she'd fly in, staying but a moment, saying little, always cheerful and laughing. Archie never found out what all the laughter was about.

Timagami in those days was little more than a fur-trading post. The population consisted of Indians, white trappers, and the odd prospector coming in for supplies. During the winter it was almost a ghost town, but in the spring, when the rivers and lakes were free of ice, the trappers with their families would come pouring in from their hunting grounds, loaded with furs. With thousands of dollars afloat in Timagami, the little town came to life in short order. People visited or gathered in noisy groups to catch up on the winter's gossip. The streets, stores, and drinking places were crowded with people in a happy holiday mood. This was Timagami as Archie first saw it.

Bill came to enquire about Archie. He stood by his bunk, smiling down, and said, 'Say boy, you're looking a hell of a lot better. I was sure you were dead when I found you lying on the shore.'

Except for a hazy memory of Bill's red head, Archie couldn't recall ever having met him. To jog his memory Bill said, 'Yeah, it was me who broughtcha here.'

Archie said, 'There's no doubt I would have died if it weren't for you and Ag-Nu. I'm terribly grateful.'

Bill raised his hand. 'Oh, forget it. Where was ya headed for?'

'Cobalt,' Archie answered, and filled him in on the details. 'And with my first earnings, I'll pay you and Ag-Nu for all the trouble I've been. . . .'

'Ag-Nu yes, me no,' said the trapper.

'But I will,' Archie insisted.

'Thanks, but forget it.'

'How far is it to Cobalt?' Archie asked.

'Around sixty miles. What do you want to go there for?'

'To work till I get enough money to get the necessary equipment to go into the woods.'

Bill eyed him quizzically. 'Woods? Oh, you mean the bush!'

'If that's what you call it, yes,' Archie said.

'What kind of bush work do ya do?' Bill wanted to know.

'None. I've never been in the woods. I haven't even been in a canoe.'

Bill's eyebrows snapped up to his hair-line. Rounding his lips, he emitted an 'Ohhhhh' so full of meaning that Archie asked what was wrong.

'Boy, you're really starting from scratch. Well, if it's bush work you want, you'll not find it in Cobalt. All you'll run into there is a pick and shovel.'

Archie frowned. 'Cobalt is the only place I know of to get work.'

'Why not stick around. There'll be lots of bush work here,' Bill advised him. 'Things will start moving in a couple of weeks.'

So engrossed in Archie's story was I that I imagined I saw Archie, Bill, Ag-Nu, and Angele emerge and move in the shadows in the snow. How long we sat looking through the window I don't know, but the fire was black out and it was freezing in Pony Hall. Shivering, Archie got up and lit the lamp. While he rekindled the fire, I asked, 'And did you get a job?'

'Yes, with the Hudson's Bay Company, freighting supplies

into their various trading-posts, north of Timagami. It was a good break for a greenhorn – that is, if he figured on spending the rest of his life in the bush. I couldn't have picked a better bunch of fellows for my first trip out. They showed a lot of patience, and they had a good laugh when I was handed a tumpline and didn't know what it was for.' He chuckled at the recollection.

'Did you see much of Bill or Ag-Nu after you got well?' I asked.

'Oh sure. Bill was on the same freighting trip, and we became the best of friends. Still are. As for Ag-Nu, I went to see him often. He was my first real contact with Canadian Indians. His absolute selflessness and kindness were amazing – he was a fine old fellow. I'll never forget him.'

'But he couldn't speak English. It must have been pretty awkward,' I put in.

'No, it's funny, but when I caught onto English spoken with a thick Ojibway accent, I discovered that Ag-Nu spoke good English.'

We laughed at this, then I asked, 'And what about Angele, the belle of Timagami?'

The rattle and noise by the stove ceased. Archie had stopped whatever he was doing. I turned and saw him staring fixedly at me. 'I married her,' he said.

Wide-eyed with interest, for I couldn't imagine Archie married, I settled myself at the table, excited at the prospect of hearing a story of love and romance. 'Hurry,' I cried, 'bring the tea and tell me all about it!'

He didn't answer. I looked to see what he was doing. He just stood there frowning.

'Are you sick or something?' I asked.

'No', he said, 'no, but I had the crazy idea – or I guess I was hoping – that you'd feel a little differently about this than you do.'

'About what?' I asked, puzzled.

He came to the table and said, 'You really don't know what I'm talking about, do you?'

'No,' I answered honestly.

'Thank you. That speaks for itself,' he said. Then he turned to go.

'What's the matter?' I called.

He wheeled around and came towards me looking like a storm. 'I'll tell you. I've been dumb . . . stupid. . . . You see, I had the foolish idea that you might come to care for me.'

'But I do care about you.'

'Oh hell,' he exclaimed irritably. 'I don't mean that kind of caring. If you cared the way I mean you'd have exlploded, caused a minor earthquake, when I said that I had got married.'

This made no sense to me so I said, 'Let's forget it.'

'No,' he said stubbornly. 'I've been waiting for the right time to tell you some things about myself that I think you ought to know, so when the occasion came I would. . . .'

He'd become hopelessly involved, and I didn't help matters by asking, 'What did you expect to come?'

'I was coming to that! Though I might as well be talking to a stump or a solid rock.' He stopped and then went on, 'I'm sorry. I lost my temper.'

'Think nothing of it,' I said. 'I get roaring mad myself – but I usually have something to get mad about.'

He chose to ignore my comment, and continued. 'From the minute I saw you, you've been crowding my mind. I had no intention of telling you till you were on the train going back home, but I guess . . .'

'What were you going to tell me, Archie?'

His expression was deathly serious, and I braced myself for some devastating news.

'To tell you that I love you.' He looked searchingly into my eyes, and I waited for him to go on, but he said no more.

'Is that all?' I asked, heaving a sigh of relief.

He winced and said, 'Yes, that is all.'

'Oh, that's nothing – the way you looked I was sure that you were going to say something.'

He promptly left the cabin, and I wondered why. He came back in a little while and seemed more himself. Seated at the table with a dish of tea before him, he said, 'Look kid, I'd like to clear up this business about Angele and me – would you mind?'

'No,' I said. 'Go ahead. But don't get mad again.'

'I won't – but you might. In telling you this I stand a chance

51

of losing you; in any case it has to be done. I married Angele and then left her in little less than a year.'

'You left her!' I gasped in disbelief.

Noting my reaction he said, 'I see that you're shocked and disgusted. I can't say that I blame you, but there you have it. What's the verdict?' He ended on a fatal note.

I didn't know what to think about this. I did feel sorry for him, he looked so miserable and embarrassed. But I wasn't as shocked or disgusted as he seemed to think I should be. 'Was she bad to you?' I asked. I guessed that this wasn't the question he expected, for he almost smiled.

'No, it wasn't anything like that. It's hard to explain without making excuses, and I won't do that. It was plain selfishness. When I discovered that I didn't like marriage, I dropped it like a hot potato. Oh yes, I had eruptions of conscience. I went back after a couple of years – it was even worse than I remembered it to be, so I left again. This time for good. In the first place, most of the old-timers in Timagami advised me against marrying her, said she was wild, and so on. A child was born seven months after we were married, if that means anything. Tommy Saville and Charlie Moore, friends of mine, went so far in trying to prevent me from marrying her that they got hold of an American clergyman who was vacationing there, to marry us, thinking that since he wasn't a Canadian citizen the marriage wouldn't be valid – I had a letter saying it wasn't. Whether the child was mine or not, or whether Angele was as wild as they say, I don't know. What I do know is that I was some kind of jerk. I stepped from under – took the easy out. There you have it.'

'Did you love her very much at first?'

'I don't know. I thought I did. You remind me a lot of my-self when I was your age. I didn't know beans about this love business. I guess I was just feeling my oats.'

That was the first time I'd heard this expression, and I asked, 'Am I feeling my oats?'

Archie laughed and said that he didn't think so.

'Good!' I exclaimed, feeling as if I had just got rid of the measles.

I was glad to see him laugh again, and I was ready for an-other long conversational bout, but he fell silent and thoughtful.

'Are you down in the dumps again?' I asked impatiently.

'No. I was just thinking,' he answered quietly.

'What were you thinking about?'

He hesitated, then reluctantly began. 'As I have already said, I didn't mean to tell you until you were leaving that I loved you, but I managed to botch it up. I guess I became unglued when you asked me about what happened to Angele – you see, I'm not proud of the hare-brained things that I've done – but I suppose I should be thankful that you're taking it all as a great big laugh. . . .'

'But, I didn't laugh – I found your story very interesting.'

'Interesting? Then I will tell you something else if for no other reason than to entertain you. When I was overseas convalescing from this damned foot and mustard gas, I met a dancer, fell in love, and married her.'

He paused to see what effect this had on me. There was plenty. In my adolescence, I had been as stage-struck as could be, and even now being with someone who had hobnobbed with a professional dancer was just too thrilling.

'Was she pretty?' I asked breathlessly.

'Pretty isn't the word. She was beautiful. She toured all over Europe, South America, and, of course, England. She was a great performer.'

By this time I was green with envy, thinking about the dancer and all the exciting places she'd been, the beautiful clothes and jewels that she must have had – the glitter of the stage.

'Yeah, before we were married,' Archie continued smugly, 'she often came with her records and costumes to dance for me.'

'Her costumes – were they nice?'

'I guess they were – what there was of them.'

'Gee, I wish I could be a dancer or an actress,' I murmured longingly. Archie left Pony Hall in disgust.

I read the account of this marriage after his death. The family of Florence Holmes, the dancer, and the Belaneys used to exchange visits when Florence and Archie were children. After Archie was wounded in the war, he stayed at his Aunt Ada Belaney's home while convalescing, and Florence, in some wartime auxiliary, often called on Archie. This led to a marriage of short duration. Florence refused to come to Canada, and Archie refused to stay in England. The marriage was annulled, so the story goes.

At this time, Archie also told me about Marie Gerard. Marie was waiting tables at the boarding house where Archie usually stayed when in Bisco. It was late September in 1914, and time for him to leave for his hunting ground. He was having an early breakfast.

He was alone in the dining-room when Marie entered with a tray full of silver that she was to put on the sideboard. Instead of doing so, she heaved the whole works towards the ceiling, and amidst the falling cutlery Marie stood laughing. By the time that Mrs. B (the owner) came dashing in from the kitchen, Archie had joined in the merriment.

Of course, Marie was fired right then and there.

Later, while Marie was packing her things, Archie tapped on her door to ask if she would like to go into the Spanish River country with him for the winter. She said that she would, and she did.

The following spring they had to go to town for more supplies before the break-up. That was the first Archie heard that there was a war on. He immediately enlisted. On his return from the war, he was told that Marie had died of T.B., and that their son, Stanley, was being ill-treated by the people he was staying with. Archie placed the boy with his friends the Langevins, where he grew to be a man.

Early the next morning, Archie came to Pony Hall, made a fire, and then awakened me. 'Hey kid,' he chirped merrily, 'it's daylight in the swamp.'

I hate cheerful people in the morning so I pretended to be asleep. He shook me, saying, 'C'mon Insect, it's time to rise and shine. Forsythe is the next stop.'

The very thought of snowshoeing forty miles was just too much.

'No, no,' I said. 'I hate this getting up so early. Besides, I've decided to stay another week.'

Silence from Archie. Then he let out a whoop. 'Let's have

something to eat,' he said – a sure sign that he was glad.

I'd made the decision to stay without giving a thought to the possibility that I might be overstaying my welcome or considering the more material matter of his having to feed me. Grub is priceless out in the bush.

I didn't know it then, but this was the trapper's busiest season. The animals, recently out of hibernation, are hungry, and they soon scent the trapper's bait and are easily caught. A sprung trap isn't a working trap, so the line must be constantly checked. Consequently Archie was always on the trail, starting early and returning at all hours of the night.

Although I was bored silly with my own company, I told Archie at the end of the week that I'd stay a little longer, but that I must be out in time to make my Easter duty.

'Just give me the word,' he said, 'and I'll see that you'll be out there on time.'

Having nothing to do and being alone so much, I was looking forward to going home. At last, in the middle of Holy Week, we were in civilization again. At Forsythe our mail had stacked up. I fumbled in my eagerness to open one of five letters. They were all from my father. I felt a pang of guilt at the realization that I'd been away for nearly two months. The thought of seeing Papa within days made me happy. But as I continued to read the first letter my eagerness waned, and when I neared its conclusion I was alarmed and puzzled, for I had never heard anything like it from my Father. He was reproachful, wondering why I wasn't coming home and telling me not to bother to answer but to step on the train and come to him at once. He continued, 'I have great faith in you, but you aren't home yet, and it is very nearly too late. I guess it is too late, except with me. You'll always be welcome where I am concerned, but I warn you that if you are not married to that man. . . .'

I handed the letters to Archie and asked him to tell me what it was all about. Archie was gravely concerned over it all. After considering the matter for what seemed like hours, he finally said that there was only one of two things for us to do. Either he would take me home immediately or we should get married.

After the long spiel from Papa, and Archie's now serious face, I became impatient. *This* was supposed to be a proposal?

55

If so it was a far cry from what I had ever expected it to be. I burst out laughing, for I thought it very funny, but for Archie it was a slap in the face.

I was angry now and said, 'What's all the fuss about anyway – you don't have to look so worried.'

'But there's plenty to worry about.'

'No there isn't. I'm just never going back home again and I'm not going to get married either.'

'Then just what do you intend to do?' Archie enquired in a most condescending manner.

In a flash I thought of Rouyn, a new mining town in northern Quebec, where a discovery of gold and copper had been made the year before. One heard or read of little else. It was a booming town with a capital BOOM. I announced calmly that I would go there and open a dance hall like those I'd read about in a book about Alaska. He was aghast at this bit of news.

Still arguing, we entrained for Senneterre, the nearest point where I could make my Easter duty. Once there, and having spent the necessary time in the confessional box unburdening my soul of its many sins, I was ready to rise and leave as soon as the Father gave me his blessing, for I couldn't take communion without that. But the blessing was not forthcoming, and we peered at each other through the window-like aperture. The Father asked me if I had told him everything.

'Yes,' I said.

'Haven't you forgotten something?' he prodded my memory. 'No.'

His voice had been gentle and persuasive, but it took on a sudden sternness as he asked the next question. 'Are you not the girl who is living in the woods somewhere with a trapper?'

'Yes, I am, and I know you too, Father,' I said, trying to place him in my memory.

His voice lifted in flaming anger, saying that I didn't know him and why did I not make a full confession in the first place.

'But I did,' I said.

'No, you did not. You didn't mention about living with a man, did you?'

'Why?' I asked, bewildered.

'Why?' he repeated, waving his arms wildly. 'Because it's wicked.'

56

'Sir, that's not right,' I said indignantly, beginning to feel temperish myself.

Because I said 'Sir', instead of 'Father', I touched off violent fireworks. He named me all kinds of a sinner before I could rise from my knees.

I scrambled to my feet and told him bitterly that if he couldn't act any better than that I didn't want an ounce of his absolution and would be satisfied with my own. I twisted my ankle in my rush to get out of the booth. He flung his door open, and in a terrible voice that resounded all through the church, he told me to get back 'in there.' But, I left in a rage, refusing even to glance back. Since this painful scene I have discovered that the good Father had a perfect right to his fury, because, as a fellow would say, 'It looks like hell from the road for a girl to be going with a man, even into God's own country, without a chaperone.'

Having no money – and less sense – to start a dance hall, I returned to Pony Hall and was glad of the chance. Once there, it was the same old routine. Archie, disgustingly busy, sharpening anything and everything that had an edge, mending snowshoe webbing, sanding the toboggan, or out on the trapline, had no time for me. One stormy night he drifted in. It was winter's last lick, and it was a dandy. He staggered in completely exhausted. I helped him off with his mackinaw and gave him a hot drink.

'Don't worry, kid,' he said, noting my concern. 'I'm O.K. Normally I'd have built a fire a few miles back, but knowing I was coming to a warm camp, I bulled 'er through.'

Supper was on the table, but tired and hungry as he was, he insisted on getting a fire going at Sunset Lodge 'to thaw that load of carcases out there'.

I told him to bring them into my cabin.

'Sure you won't mind?'

'Of course not.'

He went outside and I stood by the door. 'O.K.,' he yelled, and I held the door open as in he came with a fox under each arm. Next, he threw a sack of something through the door onto the floor, and after it he came, dragging a huge, cream-coloured animal. It was frozen in a stretched-out position and was at least eight feet long. I stared in blank astonishment as he leaned this monster, like a saw log, against the wall.

'What on earth is that?' I asked.

'Some call them Arctic wolves. Others say they're Labrador. Either way I was as surprised as hell when I first saw one.' He hung the other frozen carcases from the ceiling to thaw.

When he sat down to eat, he ate as if it were going out of style. Soon he was nodding over his plate, chewing slowly, determinedly, until an elbow slipped from the table and he all but fell into his supper.

'I feel a little groggy,' he said, straightening up. ' Would you mind if I took a couple of winks?'

I'd already cleared off the bunk, but he said that his clothes were so dirty he would lie on the moose hide. He never said 'rug'. I filled the stove as quietly as possible and went and sat at the table.

Because of the rising heat, the foxes, hanging from the ceiling to thaw, began to circle round and round and back. The melting frost on the furry coat of the wolf gleamed eerily in the shadows. I shuddered and glanced down at Archie, dead asleep on the rug. I blinked my eyes in surprise and took a good look at him. There, in the soft glow of the lamp, he seemed different from my mind's picture of him. Why he looks almost angelic, like a bronze angel, I though in wonderment. I longed to reach out and touch his face – to kiss him.

Swept by an unimaginable guilt, I turned and looked through the window. Distressed over my moment of emotion, I decided there and then to keep it a deadly secret.

As I looked into the storm I remembered Florence. Were she and Archie really happy together? My heart tightened at the thought. No! They parted, didn't they? said an inner voice. I felt better. Then, in the swirling blizzard, I imagined that I could see her dancing – dancing out there in the snow. She was happy, laughing. She sparkled like a star.

The stillness of the cabin was shattered suddenly by a bumpity-bump, and a thud that scared the daylights out of me. For an agonizing second I thought that the wolf had come to life.

'Archie!' I shrieked.

He sprang up like a shot, ramming his head into the swinging foxes. 'Wh-what's – Jees-sus – what's going on?' he shouted, half awake. The wolf carcase had overbalanced and knocked over a stand, bounced off the bunk, and crashed to the floor. We'd have had a hectic time if it had fallen on the stove.

After that night I missed Archie more and more each day that he was away. I thought that I was going straight to hell for feeling the way I did, and, as a consequence, when he returned to camp, I behaved atrociously. From such behaviour he naturally thought that I was growing to hate him, so he came to Pony Hall only at mealtimes, to make the bannock, and to restock the grub-box. Things went on this way until the spring hunt was over, and we were in Doucet.

Doucet is a little village seven miles east of Forsythe. It consisted then of about fifty families and a hotel with a store combined. Jim, the proprietor of the latter, was also a fur buyer from whom Archie had got his grubstake in the autumn. We entered the store to the cheery sounds of music, fun, and laughter.

'Well, hello, ya ole Apache.' Jim greeted us from behind the counter.

'Hi ya, Jim, How you been?' whooped Archie. He introduced me as his friend, Miss Bernard.

I noted Jim's look of puzzlement as he acknowledged the introduction. He'd known that 'someone' had been up north with Archie. I don't know what he expected, but judging from his expression I certainly wasn't it.

After the silence of the woods, my spirits rose by leaps and bounds at the sound of the uproar in the next room.

'I *hear* – the boys are in,' Archie said, grinning.

'Ya, they've been comin' in in packs. They're all here except Albert and . . . .'

Just then the door opened and in came a man with a head the size of a barrel, and shoulders to match. His shirt and trousers were stiff with oil and grime. It was impossible to distinguish the line between his face and where the dark-brown beard began. He strolled nonchalantly in, as if he'd just been across the way all winter, instead of where he had actually been – up there in the 'Land of Little Sticks' [the Barren Land].

Jim's smiling face and hearty greeting were met with a sober scowl, which immediately stamped the stranger, in my estimation, as a grouch. He waddled over to the counter and in his own good time unloaded himself and placed the bags of furs neatly in a row. He peered around for a place to spit; finding none, he did it anyhow. Finally, he spoke. 'Well, Jim' he said, still unsmiling, 'see you're still able to get around on your own hind legs, but God man, you look as though you picked yourself up by your pants and threw yourself bodily into some useless corner.' (And I thought that the man couldn't talk!)

Jim took this good naturedly, chuckling as he told Albert that that was more than he could say, as he wouldn't be able to tell what Albert looked like until he'd gone at least fifteen rounds with a bar of soap.

Albert showed neither pain nor pleasure at this repartee. He waited patiently until Jim's laughter had ceased, and then spoke.

'Say,' he said, 'can you recommend a chaser for a long-drawn-out muskrat diet?'

Before we heard what the chaser was to be, the door flew open and there stood Zed, the last of the trappers in from the hunt. He hadn't even crossed the threshold before he bellowed, 'Hi, Jim, you ol' reprobate, do you happen to have any oranges and gin?'

'Sure thing,' Jim answered.

'Fine!' roared Zed. 'Throw the oranges to the dogs and I'll have t'other meself.'

That night the boys in from the bush demanded a dance. Jim agreed, but asked what they intended to use for women, as there were few in Doucet. Somehow they managed to round up about ten, so that the dining-room, when it was cleared of furniture except for the piano and chairs, was crowded with people anticipating much fun and frolic from the jamboree. There was no shortage of musicians. The four trappers of Forsythe were there along with any number of fiddlers, and Archie could always hammer out a hot old jig at the piano.

Above the babble, the caller's bark was heard. 'Places all, for a square [quadrille]' he shouted, and the couples took their places.

The women were dressed to kill, but the men weren't so particular. There wasn't a coat in the hall. When the couples were set to go, the trappers' band struck up with the 'Devil's Dream'.

'Aliman lef', back to the right . . .' The dance was on. The din was indescribable.

The women shrieked and shouted as their partners swept them off their feet, the men 'hi-ya-ing' wildly as they stamped the floor with heavy boots in time with the music. At the end of the first change, the proprietor got down on his hands and knees and called to the rest of the men to follow in the same fashion. They made quite a spectacle – like a procession of bears parading over a hornet's nest – kicking and bucking their way from the hall. When the last one disappeared, Mr. Jim came in bearing a large tray filled with glasses of red wine, refreshments for the ladies. It was apparent on the men's return that they had indulged in more powerful stuff.

Everybody was having a rollicking good time, except me. I was given the icy shoulder by all but the trappers and Mrs. Jim – and she wasn't overly friendly, even though Archie was their customer. They had all reached their conclusions regarding me, as had the priest. Who could blame them? But at the time, I did.

Archie, at the piano, wasn't aware of what was going on. It was all bewildering to me, and after a short time I left the stuffy room and the disagreeableness behind and called Jim out. I told him I wanted a bottle of whiskey. 'What kind?' he asked. I answered that a good-sized one would do. When he brought it to me and I was in my room, I began to pour the whiskey down – at least I tried to, but it wasn't that simple; the stuff just refused to pour down. It was liquid fire. I was disappointed at this; however, with the determination worthy of a better cause, I tugged heroically at the bottle. I didn't know how much it would take to accomplish my end – to get completely 'swacked' and then go and mingle with the crowd, thus showing my contempt for them. I had no intention of saying anything to anyone, for I considered just being intoxicated sufficient insult. Sitting on the edge of the bed, I began to fear that I would never get results from the bottle. Minutes passed as I waited for something to happen, but nothing did. I supposed that I was one of those people who couldn't get drunk and decided not to wait any longer. I jumped up, with the intention of going downstairs and telling them all to go to hell.

When I got up my equilibrium went haywire. I lurched wildly across the room and had to put on the brakes to prevent crashing against a wall. I reeled and whirled dangerously around just in time to see the bed rise ceilingward at a giddy tilt. I leaped to catch it before it got out of reach. I fell, half on and half off the bed. Fingers clutching the covers tightly, I wondered sickly what on earth was happening. With the realization that I was at last higher than a kite, I started to laugh like crazy, but then suddenly I remembered that I had a score to settle. The mere thought of it and the sound of merriment from below sent my temper raging. My hostility knew no bounds, and I headed for the stairs, but wait now – I had a brilliant thought – Archie's gun, that should fix them. I made a sharp left down the dark hallway to Archie's room to get his rifle. Meanwhile, Archie had noted my absence and had begun a search. In my clumsy attempt to light the kerosene lamp in Archie's room, the globe slipped and crashed to the floor. The shattering of glass ended Archie's hunt. Bounding in from the hall, Archie shouted, 'What in hell's going on?'

'Nothing, I just wanna get your gun.'

'What on earth for?'

'Gonna sh–shoot the works,' I answered thickly.

Grasping the situation, Archie probably figured that discretion was the better part of valour, so he decided to humour me. He coughed and said, 'Of course, the gun. Yes . . . just wait a second till I get a light going here, so's I can get that jammed shell out of the breach.'

'Don't talk so much.'

'O.K., O.K., just hold your horses and I'll have this firearm loaded to kill.'

His honeyed, 'bound to please' attitude antagonized me, but I said nothing until he'd finished. I was hoping that it would be soon, because I was becoming ill. His aim was to kill time, so he feigned great seriousness and began talking again. He said,

'What puzzles me is how you're going to get rid of the bodies. They say we're right down to bed-rock – and it's awful hard to dig.'

'Oh, shut up and hurry up, or I'll get after you too,' I barked.

That is all I remember of that night.

But I shall never forget the morning after! The physical wretchedness was of little account compared to the mental and spiritual suffering. I felt defiled beyond redemption and so ashamed that I thought I'd never be able to raise my head again. I stayed in my room all day until nightfall, when Archie got a key and came in. My bags were packed and I was dressed, ready to take the west-bound train to Rouyn.

'What's this?' he demanded, pointing to the bags. 'Just where do you think you're going?'

'To Rouyn.'

This wasn't the patient Archie of Pony Hall. He hissed as he came and shook me roughly by the shoulders. 'See here! If you're going anywhere, you're going back home.' He took me by the hand in an iron grip and said 'Come on.'

We walked down the stairs and out. On the way through the jackpine woods a furious quarrel erupted over Archie's insistence on my either going back to my father or marrying him at once. After those letters from my father, I refused to talk or even think of ever going home. As to marrying, that was out of the question. I told Archie that I didn't love him. Hurt and angry, he just stood glaring at me, then he said, 'You are going home on the night train. I mean it.' I knew he meant it and so, in an ungovernable rage, I pulled his hunting-knife from his belt and struck him in the arm.

As the blood began spreading rapidly over his sleeve, I became hysterical, running and screaming from tree to tree. Finally, Archie caught up to me. One would have thought I was the injured party the way he tried to calm me down, assuring me that everything was going to be all right.

We returned to the hotel and I went up to my room. On my way up, I heard someone say that I ought to be shot. I couldn't have agreed with him more.

While I was stewing alone in my room, music, song, and laughter floated up from below. The boys were again whooping it up in style. The popular drink was a concoction of alcohol, port, and water. They mixed this together in a pail and carried it around like water wherever they went. It was called 'moose milk'. The party went on and on. Archie's voice was plainly discernible above the rest.

The third day after I had done that terrible thing to Archie, I was still in my room. During that period I hadn't eaten at all, but hunger was the least of my worries. I was more concerned about Archie – at least I thought I was. He'd knocked at the door several times, but I had refused to open it. Finally, in my desperation, I thought I had better go to Archie, tell him to cut out all that nonsense and get back into the woods where he'd be safe.

I found Archie and Ted talking and cosily sharing a pail of 'moose milk.' As soon as he saw me, Archie sprang up and shouted, 'Greetings, you're exactly what we need – it's been like a morgue in here.' Ted merely threw me a withering look and said, 'You look like a thunderstorm. What's the matter, is your knife dull?'

At this point I had the surprise of my life: Mrs. Jim invited me into her kitchen, a veritable sanctuary in a French-Canadian home. She served tea and cake. Jim joined us and we were getting on first-rate, when Mabel, the daughter, came screeching to her father, saying, 'Come and see what them damn things are doing now!' We ran to the door and there were Ted and Archie gyrating round the room, dancing to the tune of 'I Miss My Swiss' on the phonograph. Archie, his long hair and fringes flying, holding aloft a dainty sun parasol, was galloping right after Ted, who with his six-foot-four wrapped in a white tablecloth, was sprinting hither and yon like a kangaroo.

'Get my parasol,' Mabel demanded, but Jim, staring in fascination, said, 'Naw, let'em go on.'

I eventually managed to get Archie away from Ted and the 'moose milk,' and when we were alone, began to coax him to go back to the woods. His drinking worried me, and I felt that I couldn't possibly leave until I knew that he was safe.

'What difference does it make what I do?' he argued. 'You're going your way and I'm going mine.'

'Don't talk that way, Archie, please. I can't leave you like this.'

His brows lifted sceptically and he said as he rose to leave, 'All this kind benevolent consideration calls for a chaser. Have one too, you must be sick!'

Though I admitted his right to sarcasm, I broke into tears.

'Say! I believe that you mean it,' he said in surprise. There was a sardonic twist to what he intended to be a smile. Still sarcastic, he added, 'Your kindness is most touching – wishing me back in the sticks, eh? No thank you . . . I'm having a wonderful time.'

'I'll go with you,' I offered impulsively.

He took a long look at me and asked, 'Why?'

'I think . . . I love you . . .' I said with difficulty. Once it was out, I felt as though a great weight had lifted, and that whatever it was had burst into a million stars.

Archie took me in his arms. The sun had set and the dinner gong had long gone, and the time came for us to say good-night. It was far too soon for me. I was still marvelling at this new discovery. Before we parted, Archie whispered, 'We'll get the splicing business done tomorrow. Then we will start on our journey. We'll call it our wedding trip . . . into parts unknown. Romantic, eh? Just like in the story books, eh?'

But something came up and we didn't get married in Doucet after all. The next morning, hand in hand, we went to the station to get a refund on my ticket home. While I was at this, an Indian approached Archie and introduced himself. 'My name is Nuna. My people live at Lac Simon. You are the man we want.'

'You want me?' Archie repeated in surprise.

'Yes,' Nuna stated simply.

We gathered from his limited English and Archie's sparse Cree that a couple of Indians had gutted a shack belonging to two white trappers. The culprits were then in jail at Amos, Quebec, awaiting trial, and they wanted Archie to go to court as spokesman on their behalf. Their offense was a serious one, for they had not only burned down the cabin but had also flattened the stove-pipes beyond repair and dumped the trappers' winter provisions in the snow, pouring coal oil over them as well as over a bag of traps. The traps were now useless – one whiff of kerosene and your animal is headed across country. They had left shells for both shotgun and rifle to enable the trappers to shoot their food on their way out. Having neither food nor equipment left, the trappers had no choice but to head for civilization. It was fortunate for all concerned that they managed to reach the railroad.

The Indians' defense for what they had done was that these two trappers, the winter before, had polluted the country with strychnine (used as bait for wolves and foxes) and had failed to pick up the unused bait after the hunt. Consequently, the Indians lost many of their prized huskies. A dog-team to the Indian is what a car is to the businessman. When an Indian goes out in the spring, he takes his family with him, leaving no room in the canoe for the dogs, who must follow on shore, and this is usually when they pick up the strychnine. Also, these Indians were superstitious and thought that the strychnine possessed supernatural power.

Though Archie knew that it would take nothing less than a miracle to save these men from a long sentence, he nevertheless went to help them, and I remained in Doucet. It was strictly against the law for the two white trappers to use strychnine for trapping purposes, so the Indians got thirty days for their retaliation, instead of two years in jail.

The Lac Simon Indians gave Archie all the credit for this light term and, immediately after the trial, they invited him to their summer place to see if he could iron out a few troubled spots there.

We launched the canoe out of Senneterre into the Nottaway River, bound for Lac Simon, some sixty miles in. It was a lovely day, and we reached there in no time, for Nuna had a powerful outboard motor. As we entered the lake of our destination, we recognized the old familiar signs of an Indian summer encampment.

We were coming within range of the tent town, and we could see a great variety of colours flashing in the breeze. There were line upon line of clothes strung out to dry, and Hudson's Bay blankets, white, red, and green, thrown over poles to air. The women were moving about, some tanning, others washing, some dressing fish in preparation for curing, and some sitting close together sewing or gossiping – more likely both. The old women stood guard over smoky fire-places, chasing hungry huskies from the drying fish and meat. To the right, across the lake, stood the church, with the priest's house and the cemetery near-by.

A few yards from shore, Nuna veered the canoe and went straight on past a row of overturned canoes that bordered the lake. We rounded a point and came in sight of a landing. At the end of the pier stood an old Indian. Only his flowing white hair and the thinness peculiar to the aged betrayed his years, for his body was straight as an arrow, and even at that distance we were conscious of the sharp, black eyes that smouldered strangely in their deep sockets. The sun was low in the west. It tipped the treetops with gold. Beyond the stately figure in buckskins, spilled a rapid, the outlet of the lake. Flanking each side of the leaping, white water was a wall of rock, vividly and lavishly splashed with colour. The evening mists were beginning to rise. As we reached the shore the old man stood waiting to meet us. He held out his hand. Archie went forward, and they solemnly locked hands. The old man said, 'I am Papati, and I have waited for you.'

We wondered how he could have been waiting for us when no one had passed us on the way who could have told him of our coming. We put it down to the excellent running order of the moccasin telegraph.

Papati was deeply religious, but a devil when it came to laying down the law to his people. He deplored their cigarette smoking, drinking, and hobnobbing with the riff-raff in town. 'Don't talk with those I wouldn't dirty my moccasins on,' he told them and then went on, 'You are not satisfied with smoking; you have to eat it too – this tobacco they call snuts [snuff] – and when your belly is full you are as stupid as the bear after eating the worms [maggots] of a dead moose. The young women are no better. They throw their money away buying shoes with heels as long as spruce poles. On the first portage they are unable to walk, so they kick them off on the trail for their old mothers' moccasined feet to trip over . . . and they make women of their men.'

The government had sent Papati a number of horses and some farming implements. The implements Papati had stacked away as being useless, but the horses he loved. In telling of their charms and habits, the old chief reported dolefully that they didn't care for fish. Another thing that he thought utterly marvellous, at which we were supposed to show great astonishment, he recounted as follows: 'There is a man at the village who can put the straps [harness] on the horses and take them to the bush and come back with long trees of firewood. My, but they are strong.'

Papati, Archie, and I were sitting by the fire chatting when out of the calm evening the church bells rang. Papati jerked his head and said, 'It costs me twenty dollars every time it rings. He [the priest] has just come from the Barrier. They have smallpox at the Barrier, but he thinks that he is so holy he couldn't have the sickness in his mouth or his dress. But if I had been there, I would have had to stay there until the sickness passed, because I might carry it. Come, I will tell him to stay away before it is too late.'

Archie, realizing at once the danger to Papati's people, sprang up and followed him, and in the dark I caught up with them at the landing and asked if I could go too.

'Jump in,' said the chief, and soon we were cutting water in the direction of the church. The priest came forward to meet us as we landed, but when he was within ten paces of us, Papati shouted, 'Stay, come no closer. You have come from the smallpox. I tell you, do not go among my people.'

The priest stopped, peering into the darkness towards us, and then replied cuttingly, 'It's you, Papati! You forget, Papati, that if it weren't for the church, there would be no Indians. You would all have starved! Who brought the moose, the fish, and the beaver? It was the church, of course!'

'Could that be right?' Papati asked.

'No,' replied Archie, and turning to the priest he said, 'It is you who ought to be ashamed for telling such things to these people.'

'It is true!' said Father B. firmly, and turning to the chief he continued, 'You will regret this night, Papati. I am going to write to the King of Quebec!' He turned and left us standing there.

There was nothing for us to do but go home. As we walked from the landing the chief said, 'In three days I will be fifty years married to the Beaver Woman. She looks like a beaver – you think so?' We laughed, but he hurriedly added, 'She is a good woman – a very good woman.'

Papati's wife did look like a beaver, and only a short time before Archie had remarked on the resemblance.

Later, in bed in my cabin, I simply could not settle down. I was disturbed at the tiff between Papati and the priest. Then I heard Archie stir and call out to me. 'Get up,' he said. 'We're going over there and see what Father B. is up to.'

Before knocking upon the parsonage door, Archie said to me, 'Stand aside and watch him as he comes flying out.' I followed regardless. The door opened. When Father B. saw who it was, the two men stood as if frozen, sizing each other up. Finally, with a sweep of his arm, Father B. invited us inside. Smiling at us, he said, 'Entrez, entrez, I am sadly in need of company – good or bad – but you've got to be intelligent.'

Pleasantly surprised, Archie replied, 'I can't promise you that, but I confess that you've quite taken the wind out of my sails.' He flashed me a grin, adding 'I'll be damned!' This wasn't the welcome he'd expected.

After we were seated, Father B. poured wine into a glass. Handing it to Archie he said, 'This is sacramental wine. It's good for the soul – if you have one.'

That night he told us that he had wanted to be an archaeologist or a teacher of history instead of becoming a priest. 'But' he stated dolefully, 'on account of family pressure I became a man of the cloth.'

'You're still young, why don't you get out of it?' Archie asked.

'I've developed a pattern.' He stopped and added with a tinge of sarcasm, 'you would probably call it a rut.'

Archie laughed, 'Forget it, Father. I know about this "family" business. I had an aunt who vowed she would make a gentleman of me – she didn't.'

During our visit we discussed the differences between the priest and Papati. On our way back to camp Archie said, 'They are just a couple of good fellows who can't get along.'

When we arrived back at the Indian camp, we found Miranda, the chief's son-in-law, waiting for us. In French,

English, and Cree he told us that his wife, the chief's daughter, was dead.

'Don't tell Papati,' I pleaded.

'But we've got to,' Archie exclaimed.

'Yes – go,' Miranda urged.

On hearing Archie's voice, Papati got up and lit a candle. 'What is the matter, my friend?' he asked.

Archie, holding my hand, squeezed hard as he told Papati that his daughter was dead. The chief dropped the candle, and there we stood in fearsome darkness.

The day of the burial came, and as the cemetery was on the opposite shore, we launched our canoes. There were sixty canoes in the procession, all strung out, one behind the other. The old women sat silent and still as mummies, wrapped in the black shawls of mourning, and the young women had discarded their bright scarves and dresses for black or some other dark colour. The only light in this sorrow was the flashing of silver wavelets against the canoes and the glint of sparkling water from the swinging paddles as they pushed the mourners towards the graveyard.

The coffin had been lowered, and the chief, with his prayer-book in hand (besides a mass, Papati also conducted the marriage and burial services) was standing at the foot of the grave, when Miranda came, pale and breathless, his face revealing indescribable suffering. The poor fellow was taking his loss hard. He had not come across with us, for he felt that he couldn't stand to see his wife being buried, but after they had taken her away, he found that he wished to be with her to the last.

It was shortly after the funeral that Archie delivered a bomb-shell. He said, 'Tomorrow we leave. I will go on the fire-range (be a forest-ranger) and you will stay at Jim's in Doucet.'

'No! No!' I cried, for the very thought of being without him was unbearable.

'I know,' he soothed me. ' I hate the idea as much, if not more, than you do, but I must get a start on the winter's grub-stake.'

'How long will you be gone?' I asked, apprehensively.

'Two and a half months at most,' he answered.

This was too much, and I began to cry. I was weeping uncontrollably when Papati entered. Archie answered his questioning look by telling him that we were leaving in the morning.

'No,' said Papati, 'tomorrow we will bring you a wolf.'

A wolf? Just what we needed! Nevertheless we went with him and came back with four wolf pups. (The existence of the den had been known since early spring.)

A wolf, in Cree, is 'Mohingan', so we called our pup 'Hingy'. Hingy wasn't happy – but who was?

The next day the chief again reminded us of his fiftieth anniversary. 'Stay,' he said. So we stayed.

The day of the golden wedding came. We were all seated at a table made of long poles of poplar, bare except for plates, cups, and cutlery. Everyone looked expectantly at the chief. 'I am happy to see so many of you here today,' he said. 'And I thank you for your good wishes. I know that you have left your sick ones to come here, and I know that some of you have brought your sorrows locked in your hearts. I am sorry with you, for your troubles are my troubles too.'

He paused, then reminded them gently of the evils of tobacco, whiskey, laziness, etc. When he had finished his address, he turned to Archie. 'My brother,' he said, 'there is great suffering and sorrow among us. Not so long ago there were nearly ten times as many of us here. Now you see not more than a hundred. There would be more here today, but they are on their sick-bed. Maybe someone is dying right now.' (Lung and glandular T.B. were prevalent, the cause of most deaths among the Indians.) The chief, looking intently into Archie's face, pleaded, 'Could you tell us how we can take this disease from our bodies?'

Archie hesitated, thinking deeply. Finally he said, 'Outboard motors, Chief Papati, are the cause of so much sickness among your people.'

Papati stared in astonishment. Obviously he could see no sense in this answer. 'So then,' he said slowly, 'tell us the reason.'

'It is because' continued Archie, 'after you have made many trips over a portage with heavy loads on your backs, you become overheated. And then, before you cool off, you jump into the canoe and start the motor, and there you sit with no movement to keep you warm. From the speed of the canoe, water is sprayed over you, the wind is blowing through your wet clothes. No, I don't like motors,' Archie ended.

'That sounds true,' said Papati, 'but there must be some other reason.'

'Yes,' Archie replied. 'You people do not eat the right things.'

'But we have lots to eat,' interrupted the chief.

'Yes, yes, I know; but besides meat, fish, and beans you ought to have greens and, most important, you should have lots of butter, eggs, and milk.'

'This is very much to have,' said Papati with despair.

'Yes,' acknowledged Archie. 'But it would be a great help in fighting disease if you could have these things – if only during the summer months.'

'But there is nothing like that here,' Papati cried, showing his empty palms.

'You could have it if you would grow it,' said Archie.

'But the Indians don't know how,' the chief argued.

'Perhaps you could learn.'

'I don't know,' Papati murmured doubtfully.

'Someone would be only too glad to show you, I'm sure,' insisted Archie.

The chief shook his head gloomily. 'No, I'm afraid not, because we Indians cannot speak French, and that is all everybody speaks.'

This flimsy excuse revealed to Archie that farming as a cure for T.B. was as much dreaded by these people as the disease itself. He went about it more diplomatically. 'Maybe' he ventured smoothly, 'there is a man among you who knows something about gardening?'

'I don't think so,' said Papati, somewhat uncomfortably.

'But you might find one if you ask,' Archie persisted.

'And if I found one, what would I ask him?' enquired the chief guardedly.

Then Archie, to whom I knew the very thought of tilling the soil was revolting, began talking like Alpha of the Plough. I listened in amazement, for he was elaborating in the most convincing manner on the virtues of gardening. 'Should you find the right man,' he said, with shining eyes, 'he would be only too glad to settle, with his family, on a good piece of land.'

'Maybe there is not very good ground here,' Papati stated, a little too hopefully.

'Oh, yes,' Archie said, drawing a deep breath. 'Once the land is cleared, you'll have the finest garden in the country. Of course you understand that you will all have to turn to, to help clear the land, but after that the rest is up to the man who does the farming.'

Papati, who was well-nigh beaten, mused that Indians were trappers.

'Oh, yes, that reminds me,' Archie rushed on, still intent on his argument, 'you will have to buy everything from the man who works the land, because he will be unable to hunt as well as tend to his garden, so it is only from what he grows that he will get any cash.'

'But the Indians like to hunt better,' replied the chief desperately.

'That may be,' Archie went on firmly 'but the farmer will live a much better life than the trapper.'

Papati blurted the truth at last. 'The Indians', he said flatly 'do not like farming.'

'I can't see why,' Archie went on persuasively, 'for it is a much easier life.'

Shafts of light sparkled in Papati's eyes and a Satanic smile played about his lips as he said, 'Then, my brother, why don't you change your hard life for one that is easier, and the Indians will pay you well for it!'

Archie's shock at this boomerang was noted by all, and he scarcely had the time to tell them that he didn't like farming either, before the place was in an uproar of hoots and shouts of laughter.

When Papati could be heard, he said, 'Well, that will be enough gardening for one day,' and everyone applauded agreement. This unexpected diversion had made the people forget their troubles temporarily, and they now chatted together in a light-hearted manner. Several women approached our table with huge platters of steaming food – a most welcome sight. The fare consisted of fried fish, moose steaks, young partridges, and ducks. For dessert there were sweet patty-cakes and raisin dumplings, among many other things.

But we were not to eat just yet, for Papati, his old, wrinkled face smiling, was on his feet demanding attention. Glancing towards Archie, he began to speak. 'Just now my friend spoke to me, and he told me that if he and Anahareo can have our blessing and love, it will make their lives together more happy.

'They are good and every one of us loves them. Now, together, we will pray to God and ask him to keep the black clouds of sickness and sorrow from their trail and make their hearts and their souls shine with truth and happiness while they are living, and afterward, in the Other World.'

While all heads were bowed in prayer, the chief reached out and solemnly joined Archie's hand in mine across the table. My thoughts raced back to Mary Robinson and Kanistonou. When the prayer ended, Archie and I bowed our thanks to the good people, and Archie again congratulated the old man on his long and happy life with the Beaver Woman. 'Fifty years from today, Chief Papati,' he said, 'Anahareo and I will spend our golden wedding at this very spot.' There was no doubt in our minds but that we would.

And so this is how and when Archie and I were married.

/\.\/.\/.\/.\/.\

We left Lac Simon the following morning. By the time we reached Senneterre it was agreed between us that I would go to Rouyn while Archie went fire-ranging farther east. Now that I was actually going to Rouyn, which meant our living apart, I found myself heartily wishing that the town had never been built. I packed reluctantly, and without Archie's encouragement it wouldn't have been done at all. That was his way: once a thing was decided upon, it must go through. He went in search of a crate for Hingy, as I was taking him with me. I had to hurry now to get dressed or I would never make the train. I slid into a pair of black breeches, a green shirt, and high-cut boots. I decided to wear a spotted sealskin vest instead of a hunting-shirt. I had no doubts whatsoever as to what the best-dressed waitress should wear. This was the type of work I meant to look for.

I took a last look at our camp and walked with leaden steps up the trail. Archie carried my luggage – a pack-sack and a crate of wolf – to the depot. I guess most everybody has had his heart-breaking good-byes. I only hope that others have been able to take theirs more bravely than I did mine. That very afternoon Archie would step into a canoe, loaded to the gun-wales, and head northward to some place in that vast Ojibway country. I felt that once he was in there I would never be able to find him.

After a seeming eternity I found myself standing on the station platform at Rouyn. It was dark and raining. Prospectors, business men, and delivery boys, rushing hither and yon, pro-vided much activity. With the pack on my back and poor Hingy in his crate at my feet, I just gazed about in bewilder-ment. Thus stood the would-be dance-hall girl, gambling-den runner, or keeper, or something.

The townsite was two miles away, so I had to take a cab. As the driver handed Hingy to me, he asked, with an accent a mile wide, 'Ees 'ee a 'Osky?' [Husky]. 'No, it's a wolf,' I answered, causing him to drop Hingy's crate to the ground with a bang in his sudden fright. I just about ate that taxi-driver raw, but his profuse apologies won me over to the point of my per-mitting him to tie the crate to the bumper.

As we bounced about over the rough, muddy road, I tried to get across to the driver that I wanted a hotel that was re-spectable, but inexpensive. I was being very cautious, remem-bering Archie's horror at the thought of a mining town.

At the end of our journey, when I lifted Hingy's crate from the bumper, it was empty! Hingy was gone. Bouncing over the rutted road had knocked the lid off. 'Backtrack,' I demanded of the driver, but we could find no trace of Hingy on the way back to the station. Heart-broken and furious, I ran up to the depot wicket and asked the station agent if he had seen a wolf. Peering over his spectacles, the agent gave me an odd look and said, 'No, lady, I haven't seen a wolf in years.' I entertained little hope of ever finding my pet alive. What a night!

The next day I dragged myself up the street to look for work. I stopped at a 'Waitress Wanted' sign in a window. I went inside, but my courage failed me when it came to applying for the job. I ordered a meal instead, but I couldn't eat. Hunched over a cooling dinner, I must have made a picture of dejection, for with an expression of alarm on his face the proprietor came over and asked with great concern what was troubling me. He was a Finn, a large, blond man with the kindest eyes I have ever seen.

I said lamely, 'I came because of that sign in the window.'

He looked puzzled for a moment, then exclaimed, 'Oh, about the waitress. . . .'

'Yes.'

'Y-you are a waitress?' he stuttered, looking still more surprised, since I certainly looked anything but. Manfully he regained his poise and said cheerfully, 'Good! Now, don't feel bad anymore. You just come right over here and work.'

I thanked him hurriedly and dashed madly to the hotel to have a good cry. When I reached my room, a newspaper reporter stood at my door. It wasn't long before he was sitting and listening, sympathetically, to my woes. When I had finished, he promised to print a whole pile of notices about Hingy's disappearance and tack them up all over town. Thoughts of those notices gave me faith to believe in Hingy's return, and I went to work comforted.

There was quite a write-up in the next edition of the *Northern Miner*. The reporter had made the story a real heart-breaker. He also named the place where I should be contacted in case Hingy was found, and, as a consequence, Mr. Ring's restaurant did a booming business. Everyone wanted to see the 'waitress wolf-girl'.

I was working the midnight to eight shift, several days after, and had gone to bed when Mr. Ring banged at my door, shouting excitedly that Hingy had been found. Like a shot I leapt out of bed and ran down to the lobby, yelling, 'Where is he, oh where is Hingy?' I fully expected him to be there, but he wasn't. Then Mr. Ring was pushing me up the stairway, telling me that I had better go and put some clothes on, for I was still in my pyjamas. I dressed and went down in search of the man who had said that he knew about Hingy, but he had already gone. I was a jumping idiot by the time someone at last told me that the wolf was under a meat-storage warehouse, some six blocks away. Hingy, no doubt, had smelled the meat and had gone there to get something to eat, and it was there that I found him, sort of jammed under the low building. I called him several times, but he wouldn't come until I had talked to him several minutes. I carried Hingy to my room and put him on the bed, and there he lay looking at me in such a way that I knew he remembered me.

Knowing that he probably hadn't eaten for eight days, I dashed down to the kitchen for a steak and a bowl of milk. He was off the bed and cowering in a corner when I returned. After some coaxing he drank the milk, but in his half-starved condition it took him some time to eat the meat.

I knew that we, Hingy and I, would have to go and try to find Archie before anything else happened, but I had to stick to my job till they found a replacement for the dining-room. That took three days. Hingy was beginning to perk up; in fact, he had perked up enough to chew up one of my shoes. When they found my replacement I lost no time in packing and getting a crate for Hingy, and then we were bound by train for Oskelaneo, Quebec, 350 miles east. Hingy had to ride in the baggage car. Four hours later, when we changed trains, I was allowed to see Hingy. He was terribly unhappy. All I could do was give him water, then back into the baggage car he went.

We arrived at our destination after what seemed a million hours. Of course the first move was to get Hingy out of that crate, but when I lifted the lid and saw Hingy just lying there, not moving, I thought he was dead! It was dark by that time, but fortunately the hotel was near by. I took Hingy up, ran to the hotel, rushed up to the man at the desk, and said, 'I need a room quick. My wolf is sick.' The man was startled to say the least, and just stood there. 'Please hurry,' I urged. Without a word he led me upstairs to a room. Hingy was really ill. 'I must get a doctor,' I said in panic, but I had no luck. Why, of course, a warm mustard bath, one of Grandma's remedies. The desk clerk was most helpful and kind in helping me to acquire the dry mustard and the wash-tub; but Hingy didn't respond. He died in the early morning.

Hingy was gone, but that didn't mean the end of my troubles. I had to find out where Archie was located, then see if I would be allowed to go to him; and if permitted, then get someone to take me in.

My first move was to go to the chief ranger's office, for even in my confused state of mind, I knew that that was Archie's headquarters. But, right off the bat, the chief shot off a string of rules a mile long against wives joining their husbands on the fire-range. I had been crying earlier, as I had just buried Hingy, and now that I was apparently going to be refused permission to see Archie, I knew that I was about to cry again. It was then that the chief patted my shoulder and said, 'Never mind, you can go to your husband – not only that, I know of someone who will take you right there! Now, smile.'

As a fire-ranger out of Bisco, Archie had patrolled his territory by canoe, but here he'd been consigned to an eight foot by eight foot look-out tower. He hated being confined to that cubby hole, as he called it; besides, his fear of heights amounted to a phobia. It took all the willpower that he possessed to climb the 106-foot ladder, and he found it more frightening to climb down. Even if they had given him a water route, Archie would still have been out of his element, because this was the era of the outboard motor.

However, the main thing was that we were happy to be together again. Nothing out of the ordinary happened during the first of that summer. Archie tanned hides and I made mitts, moccasins, leggings, and a shirt from them. By the time his work with the Forestry Department was finished and we returned to Doucet, our outfits were ready for the winter.

Back in Doucet, after poring over dozens of maps of northern Quebec, Archie finally decided on going into the Jumping Caribou country for the winter. Before we started, he said 'We'll just keep going until freeze-up forces us to build.'

This was my first serious canoe trip; all the others until then had been of a frivolous nature. I soon found, to my disgust, that there is a vast difference. The correct canoe procedure is to keep the strokes, bow and stern, in perfect unison and to be quick on the recovery – which means you must throw the paddle *smartly* forward at the end of each stroke. Keep going, in other words. Ignorant of all this, I often stopped, letting my paddle drag in the water while I turned to talk to Archie. Thus I committed two unforgivable sins in less time than it takes to tell.

At last Archie said, 'It's nice of you to want to help, but if you insist on talking and don't keep time with the paddle, I'd much rather you sat in the bottom of the canoe.' This dampened my spirits, for I really wanted to be a part of the expedition. When we came to the first portage I naturally expected to help carry some of the load, but as I picked up a pack-sack Archie said, 'Oh, oh, don't touch any part of the load. Here's the tea-pail and tomahawk, you can take these across.'

Archie abhorred the sight of a woman doing a man's job. 'It's the surest way to emasculate a man,' he swore. I sat on a rock and looked sad, hoping this would make him relent, but instead I saw a smile whisk across his face, making me so angry I didn't know what to do until my wandering gaze rested on the canoe. This was my chance to show him!

I launched the canoe and headed for the centre of the river, about fifty yards out. I stood up in the canoe to see what was 'cooking' below. There was plenty. I realized too late what an idiot I was for getting myself into this predicament. Even Archie, an expert, wouldn't have run these rapids before studying them well. He could tell by the drop of the land that this would be a swift and dangerous rapid to run. Now I was at the head of the rapids where the black water seemed to stop and meditate on what course to take. The canoe jerked viciously towards the foaming water below, and suddenly I was in the thick of it.

Lashing tongues of water curled and flayed high above the leaping canoe, jagged rocks loomed ahead, hundreds of them! I was in it but good, and I was frightened and sorry. Suddenly I found myself at the foot of the rapid, circling dizzily in an eddy, a fool for luck.

My weight alone had pulled me through. Since I was very light – I weighed only 111 pounds – the canoe had floated down like a chip. I didn't use the paddle, because I didn't know where to put it. I was still gasping for breath when Archie appeared at the landing. His reaction to my prank was beyond description. It showed him, at least, that I didn't intend to stay put, and when he recognized that I was intent on learning about the bush, he was more than patient in teaching me.

We made the seventy miles to the Jumping Caribou River without incident. It was hard work and, as usual, a rush trip – a cabin had to be built and a hundred and one things accomplished before the mink hunt could begin. Once the trapping season did start, it was the same old show as at Sunset Lodge – Archie away all the time.

I was in love, so this did not bother me as it had the last weeks at Pony Hall. Still, there was nothing to look forward to but waiting for Archie to come home from his trap-lines. I grew restless. Noting this, Archie tried to create a diversion and started a little game. He wrote a number of notes, which he put into several tins – tins in which we kept our groceries – and then hid them in the most unlikely places about the cabin. When I got up in the morning, I would find a note on the table which read: 'You are an awful little beast and I hate you! No, no, I don't mean that. Look into the tea tin and find out what I really do mean.' The tea tin's message stated: 'So sorry, so sorry, my back-breaking apologies. I haven't decided yet what I mean. Look in the mustard can.' This note merely added, 'It smells too awful in here. Think I'll go into the rice pail.' So I'd go on a treasure hunt until I found the prize – a letter. Boy, how that man could write. He had such delightful games, and he simply spilled over with surprises.

One morning, lying on the bunk, hating to get up and face another lonely day, I had an idea. We would build a bungalow in the jackpine flats by the shore of Atik Lake. It would be a place we could call home. I flew out of bed and with pencil and paper, architect me made a plan of the new cabin. It would be chock-full of rustic furniture, which I would make, and would have a fireplace, which I would build. I had no doubt that I could – I had watched Papa making furniture and fireplaces, and it had looked so simple.

I couldn't wait to share with Archie this wonderful plan of mine. He came home that night, and I was so absorbed in telling him about it that I didn't notice how he was receiving the idea. Not until I had run myself empty of words did I notice his expression of horror. I asked him what was the matter, and he answered, 'I'm sorry, kid. Please don't feel bad, but you've just lit on my pettiest of pet aversions. The very thought of a permanent establishment gives me a feeling of suffocation. Let's not even think about it.'

I was hurt, and it was painful to see my dream bungalow fade away. But soon I had another notion. This time I would be more diplomatic. I drew picture after picture of babies – babies with big noses and bony knees like Archie's, carrying axes and guns. Some were on snowshoes, and others in canoes, some were dressed in buckskins and some in frilly bonnets of blue. (I printed 'blue' on the bonnets.) Archie was amused at the drawings, but he didn't take the hint. Bluntly I asked, 'Why can't we have a baby like everyone else?'

'I was wondering when you were coming to that,' he said quietly. 'The answer is no.'

'No what?' I asked.

'NO BABIES.'

It was the day before Christmas, and I was feeling sorrier for myself than usual when Archie came in. 'Heavens,' I gasped in surprise, 'it's still daylight. What happened?'

'Nothing. Hurry up and jump into some clothes, we're going up the ridge and get some meat and suet from that moose I got the other day.'

'But we still have meat here,' I said.

'Yeah – but no suet.'

I didn't know then that a Christmas pudding was a must with Archie.

On our return trip from the ridge, I managed a slick disappearing act. It was dark as we went down a steep side-hill. I slipped and, in trying to regain my balance, I staggered off the trail, stumbled and fell head-first under a spruce. There was little snow beneath the branches, so it was a seven-foot drop. With the weight of the pack on my back, it was no trick at all to get through the maze of limbs, but my snowshoes tangled and caught in them, and there I hung, suspended upside down. I heard Archie shouting, 'Where are you?'

'Down here,' I yelled back.

'What in the hell are you doing down there?' he laughed.

I forgot and forgave when, back in camp, he began the building of the pudding. Before we went to get the suet, Archie had put the dried fruit into a pot of water to soak, and it was now ready for the project. Archie beamed with fun and good cheer, but I was blue. This was my first Christmas away from home. In an attempt to lighten my spirits, Archie put me to work.

'Hey, honey, how'd you like to give me a hand?' he asked.

'All right, what do I do?' I asked listlessly.

'Just squirt the stones out of the prunes, while I get busy and line up the ammunition [the ingredients].'

My assignment wasn't in itself bad, but the prunes were mixed in with the dried apples and raisins, so I had to wallow in the pot up to my elbows. I resigned myself to this messy chore and a long, dull evening. But I was wrong. At first I didn't know whether to laugh or not, but I thought it odd when I saw Archie, with such loving reverence, extricate a hunk of suet from the pack-sack, and then, rolling his eyes in ecstasy, breathe in its aroma. He stood as if enchanted; then the mass of suet slipped from his hand, snapping him from his rapture. He caught it with surprising alacrity, only inches from the floor. Acting the neurotic chef, caressing a non-existent moustache, etc., he started the pudding. He had been putting me on.

He dearly loved spices – he must have bought them by the crate. There was cinnamon, nutmeg, ginger, cloves, chili, and curry. Judging from the 'heat waves' rising from the bowl, he must have used them all. The pudding was hotter than hell. Anyhow, because of the fun we'd had, the best part of the pudding was in the making. And he made not one, but several, boiling them in sugar bags he'd begun to save in the early autumn.

/\.\/.\/.\/.\/.\/\

I was in love with a trapper, and a life in the woods lay before me. Unless I was prepared to vegetate in the cabin from October to May, I knew I must find something to do. Trapping, of course, was the only choice, but I thought of the marten that Archie had killed. Could I bring myself to do that? Why couldn't I? There were slaughter-houses by the millions. We are all part of killing. Perhaps I could do it if I tried hard – tried real hard. Thus I argued with myself, and finally I did learn to trap. How I wish I hadn't! The fact that I hated to kill and my ever-present remorse over this now will never right the wrong. I can still hear the screams of the suffering animals – the mink, marten, fisher, lynx. I still see the poisoned foxes and wolves lying on the frozen lakes, and the drowned beaver and otter at the bottom of the lakes and streams.

It was in March, 1928, my second season of trapping that I came upon a lynx in one of my traps. Judging from his tracks he'd been there all of ten days. The weather hadn't been cold enough to put him out of his misery. He had stripped the bark from everything within his reach. The only thing that kept him alive was eating snow. I would have let him go, but he was in too poor a condition. He had gnawed at his trapped paw until the bones were bare of flesh.

This was the end! I vowed that I would never trap again.

Archie continued the hunt, and for me the time now dragged. What now, I wondered. Was this to be my way of life then? The thought was unbearable as was the alternative – to leave Archie. I'd had a taste of that when I went to Rouyn.

At last the spring hunt was over. Archie asked me if I would like to go with him to pick up the last of his traps. I was only too glad of the chance to leave and be relieved of the monotony of camp. And that was when we got two live kitten beaver. The mother had been caught. She'd cut the anchor line and made off with the 'drowning-stone' and the trap, to die at the bottom of the pond. We searched but never found her, so it was a dead loss all around.

Kitten beaver are unable to remain under water for any length of time, so these two were easily caught. I lifted them from the pond and put them inside my shirt, and there they stayed without a sound or movement.

When we got back to camp, Archie emptied the grub-box and made a bed of moss and leaves. When I put the beaver in the box, they crawled shakily to a corner, huddling together, holding each other with their little hands. We covered them over with a towel and walked quietly away.

I was worried and anxious as to whether the kittens would live, or die like one that an Indian had once brought to Jim. Of course, that baby beaver had scarcely a spark of life when it was dumped from a sack onto the hotel floor. In an attempt to revive it, I had put it in a tub of water, but this hadn't helped. We had also tried to feed it milk, but due to the peculiar shape of a beaver's mouth it had been impossible to spoon-feed it. The beaver has a mouth within a mouth, an upper lip that covers the long, chisel-like teeth used in cutting down trees, and an inner apparatus that is, in fact, the real mouth.

Though it was beyond our power to save that little beaver, we had stayed with it until it died. I meant to bury it by the lake, but when I returned to it after a few hours of sleep, the beaver was gone. To my enquiry, Jim said, 'When I seen it was dead, I threw it in the slop-pail.' I went to my room and cried.

I was determined that nothing like that would ever happen to the two mites that we had just brought home. I loved them and meant to keep them. It wouldn't be easy to get Archie to agree to this, because his fur catch was small, and to make it harder for me to have my way about the little creatures was the fact that a man in eastern Quebec had started a beaver farm, making beaver more valuable alive than dead.

Wanting to discover just how difficult it was going to be, I said, 'They're sure going to make great pets, aren't they?'

'Pets?' questioned Archie.

'Yeah, them.'

'Pets nothing,' he stated, 'we're selling them to Jim. There's a good price for live beaver.'

And that was supposed to be the last word on that! I was boiling. 'Oh no,' I said, 'Jim will never get these!'

The argument that erupted then showed no signs of ending until morning, but we were interrupted by a sound from the box. Instantly we were at their side, and there they were, standing on hind legs, with upraised arms, looking straight at us. It was quite obvious that they were looking to us for help. Instead of quarrelling, we should have been planning a diet for them. We were at a loss until Archie remembered that there was some tinned milk under the bunk. The brand of milk, which Jim had given us by mistake, was sweet and sticky, the consistency of honey – just fine, since it didn't spill easily. In spite of our unsuccessful attempt with the beaver in Doucet, we tried feeding these with a spoon, but again to no avail. I was in tears. Then Archie exclaimed excitedly, 'Say, this stuff is sticky enough to stick to a stick! We'll poke it into them!' And this we did. I held the inner mouth open while Archie thrust in a glob, pulled out the feeder, and quickly clamped the jaws shut. They caught on to it in no time.

The next morning, Archie decided that we should pack and

leave for Doucet. I hated the idea of going, because the sooner we reached there, the sooner the showdown would come concerning the kittens.

'Let's put it off for awhile,' I suggested hopefully.

'Sorry – we can't. We haven't the grub. As it is, we'll have to shoot and troll for our food.'

We packed. Everything was in the canoe but the beaver. I'd cleaned out the 18" x 40" camp stove, which was to be used as a crate. But when we looked into the pen, there was only one kitten. We searched for hours without success. I was sick with worry for fear that Archie would leave before we found it, but I needn't have worried. He was still searching after the sun went down. It was nearly dark when I heard him shout.

My first thought was of him. Was he hurt? Had he broken a leg, his back, his head? Filled with foreboding I simply flew the distance between us. His constant hooting and shouting directed me to him.

'I've got him. I've got him,' he yelled triumphantly from behind a thick growth of willows. I crashed through, regardless of the rips and tears to my breeches. There was Archie, up to his neck in a muskeg creek, holding a willow in one hand and in the other, a flapping, splashing beaver. 'Hurry, hurry,' Archie yelled. 'Quick, he's slipping from my grip.'

Instead of doing as he said, I grabbed him by the wrist and hung on for dear life. I was terrified, afraid that he might lose hold of the willow and drop from sight. Those harmless-looking muskeg creeks are highly dangerous. Usually they are only about eight feet wide, some even less, but just two feet below the surface, there's a seemingly bottomless mass of black, soupy ooze. Like quicksand, once you get beyond your depth there's no hope of getting out. So I had cause to panic, to say nothing of the fact that Archie couldn't even swim!

Though he knew the treacherous nature of these creeks, he bore no trace of apprehension and merely wanted me to take the beaver. At last, reluctantly, I took the kitten and left him there to pull himself out. I was scolding the beaver for causing so much trouble and worry, when Archie made his appearance. He was a dreadful mess, plastered to the armpits with black, greasy muck. I wouldn't have blamed him for being angry; indeed, I expected it. But he just gave me a sheepish grin, glanced down at his plaster job, and said, 'Well, isn't that a son-of-a-bitch.' It was, and we both laughed.

Although we had been packed up to leave, Archie decided after the muskeg episode that we could stay in the bush a while longer.

Since the day after we had brought the beaver home, Archie had been away most of the time, so he and the kittens, whom we called McGinty and McGinnis, were practically strangers when he returned to the camp. I, on the other hand, had been with them constantly and had grown to know and love them. They were affectionate – so cuddly and lovable. What a difference they made to my life in the woods. The Macs awakened at 5 p.m. and from then on they were busy beaver, eating, splashing in their bath (the wash-tub), and carting fire-wood all over the place. They never tired of wrestling. They explored and inspected everything, then they'd come to me to play or to be petted. They cried only when I was out of sight, so I had to sleep on the floor. Ironically, I'd given up all hope of having a baby, only to be suddenly presented with twins! Minus the diaper routine, their needs were no different than that of an infant. In this case diaper-changing would have been easier than emptying the bath tub every time they 'went'; beaver have to be in water when they go to the toilet.

Archie hadn't brought up the fate of the beaver since the night of the big quarrel, and this silence worried me, since I knew that once Archie had made up his mind about anything, it was useless to discuss it further.

We started the journey to Doucet. The first day was some-thing awful. From the very instant that they were put into the stove, the beaver kicked up a ruckus. Their wailing, crying and squealing was nothing compared to the scraping and raking of tooth and nail – hammer and tong as it were – on the metal stove. You can imagine what this did to Archie, who couldn't even bear talking on a trip. The first thing he said when we pulled ashore that night was 'I'd rather paddle steady for a whole month than listen to that for a second.'

While Archie was unloading the canoe, the Macs were whooping it up in the stove. I didn't dare let them out for fear of their getting away. Archie said, 'I suppose I'll have to make another pen for those little buggers. This time it's going to be strong enough to hold a water buffalo.'

We spoke few words that night, but just before going to bed Archie patted my arm and asked, 'Why so glum? Cheer up, we'll soon have lots to eat.'

Eat? If that were all I had on my mind, I'd have been happy.

The closer we came to Doucet, the more nervous I became. I wanted so badly to keep McGinty and McGinnis. At dawn we were awakened by the Macs. Not only had they broken out of their pen; they had also found the lake, had a jolly good swim, and then came begging us for something to eat! It used to be beaver-trapper Archie who 'snuck up' on beaver. Quite a switch to have them sneak up on him! He was dumbfounded.

I set about preparing their food (to stretch out the milk supply, they were having it diluted, with porridge), and Archie examined their pen to see what could be done about it. When the Macs had finished eating, they began to comb their coats (they have a special claw for this). I volunteered to look after them, so Archie returned to bed. He had no sooner tucked himself in than one of the beaver went over and propped himself against Archie's side and continued with his combing.

Archie gave me a startled look and then grinned. When the little fellow had finished his combing, he ambled close to Archie's face, sniffing and poking about. He nibbled a little at his eyebrows, and then, with a great sigh, he settled himself on Archie's chest and fell asleep.

'I'll be darned,' said Archie, amazed.

I was so happy, for I thought, who in heaven's name would throw his bedfellow to a big, bad fur-buyer?

After a little Archie whispered, 'Those fellows are bound to sleep all day, so let's get going.' So we started off once more.

We caught on to their routine pretty quickly. They had breakfast in the evening and stayed round until the tent was up – they loved activity. Our suppertime was their playtime. They had to sample everything on our plates; then off they'd go to the lake, and we'd follow to watch the fun. They adored an audience and would roll and birl and whack with their funny little flat tails, wrestling and diving, showing off for all they were worth.

At dawn they would return to the tent and play 'nosey' – cold, wet nosey. They were great fun, and, as I had hoped, the two Macs won Archie over completely. But he still said nothing about keeping them. He only looked more determined, I thought, as I left him by the fire and went to sit by the lake. This was the last night of the journey. Tomorrow – Doucet and the battle. My mind was a jumble of dread, fear, and anger. I had visions of wrestling Mac and Mac at gunpoint from a fur-buyer.

'C'mere,' Archie called.

Well, here it comes, I thought, and braced myself for the worst. His expression was heartening, but I was still suspicious. He made a place for me beside him and said, 'I'm sorry, Old-timer, I didn't mean to be cruel. I just didn't know that they were . . . like that – those beaver of yours.'

Oh, imagine my relief and joy – I could keep them!

We arrived, finally, on the shore of Lac Attic, a scant mile from the hotel and our grubstake debt. Still mistrustful, I told Archie to go to town by himself, and I would stay and take care of the Macs.

'Yeah,' he agreed. 'In case our catch doesn't cover the bill, that might be a good idea.'

Fur had dropped in price, and after we kept out $300 for ourselves, we still owed Jim $80.

There is whoop-la in plenty in northern whistle-stops like Doucet when the Indians and white trappers come in from the hunt. Springtime is funtime. Everybody is in a holiday mood, and money and 'moose milk' flow like water. Because of the beaver, we had to camp by the lake. Jim came to see Archie one night, and following the usual greetings he said, 'Say, Archie, want to do me a favour?'

'Sure Jim, what is it?' asked Archie.

Jim hesitated, then went on. 'It's this way, ya see. I think I'm gonna run out of booze, and I'm scared they'll [the police] get wise if I keep sending for the stuff by the barrel like I'm doin'. Look – I got a hell of a good recipe and the whole dang shebang [a still] for making hootch. Do you think you could run the rig for me?'

'Oh sure, Jim,' said Archie. 'I'm an old hand at that. I used to make the odd batch for myself – and for any of the guys that happened along while she was still steaming.'

'Good!' said Jim. 'You'll have your bill paid off, and then some.'

'Oh hell,' Archie interrupted, 'forget it. I said I'd do you a favour and that's it.'

So Archie made booze for Jim while waiting to start another summer as fire-ranger. It was a ten-day, or a one-batch, wait.

Archie had chosen a look-out tower rather than the patrol, so we could remain stationary for the beaver's sake. It was a happy and pleasant summer, the best that I can remember, but when the leaves began to turn, in the early fall, Archie became more and more withdrawn and went about as if he alone carried all the cares and woes of the universe.

I suggested that he go to Senneterre and see a doctor. He looked at me and said, 'Don't be silly, there's not a darned thing wrong with me.' Yes, he was irritable too. I put it down to worrying over not having a hunting ground in mind yet, for the coming winter. He knew there was nothing to gain by going back into the Marque, our last trapping ground, or to the Jumping Caribou country, because they were both almost depleted of fur-bearing animals.

It was less than a week before it was time to leave the tower and the job when I saw Archie coming down the trail, and the moment I spied him I knew something was up. Although his expression was serious, the worried look that had caused me so much anxiety was gone.

'Well,' he said as he approached me, 'we've got a new job.'

Thinking that he'd just got information over the phone in the tower, I asked excitedly, 'Where is it? What kind of a job?'

'I'm off the beaver hunt – for good.'

His answer didn't make sense. What connection was there between a new job and being off the beaver hunt? Of course, I didn't believe him. 'I only wish you meant that,' I said, and went into the cabin to prepare supper. He followed.

'It's true. I'm through.'

I searched his face to see whether he was serious or this was a joke.

It was no joke. Of this moment, Archie wrote in his *Pilgrims of the Wild*: 'I am now the President, Treasurer and sole member of the Society of the Beaver People. How about a donation?'

He had had time to think this all over, but I certainly wasn't prepared for this good news, and it struck me like a hammer. I can't remember exactly what I said. I had hoped many times that he would quit trapping beaver, but I never thought he would.

'What will you do now?' I questioned.

'That's a good question – but let's not worry about the answer. My idea is we could start out easy, say with a family of beaver – and ours – and then maybe later on . . . somehow. . . .' Jumping ahead of himself, he continued. 'Do you know, I wish I could repopulate the country with beaver again, or at least try to keep them from dying out altogether. Do you like the idea? Are you game?'

I was. Enthusiastically so.

This decision wasn't made on the spur of the moment. He'd been troubled all summer with the choice of beaver trapping or becoming non-supporting, even destitute. Beaver skins were his main source of income. McGinty and McGinnis were, of course, responsible for the change in Archie, but where or when had they sown the seed? I think McGinnis had staked his claim the morning he first poked his cold, wet nose into Archie's face, and this playful act had irrevocably changed the course of a man's life.

Although I knew the fire-ranger job was just for the summer, I cried the day Archie was told, over the phone, that it was over. How I hated the thought of leaving! And poor Mac and Mac – they must leave their house too. They actually had one, for those clever little fellows had dug a den for themselves in the bank of the lake. They slept there during the day. Now they were in the process of building a house of sticks and mud on the top of their den. They even had the beginnings of a feed-raft anchored in front of their dwelling. They knew exactly what they were doing and worked like 'real beavers' all summer.

The worst part of leaving was that we didn't know where we were going. We knew only that we were going in search of a family of beaver with which to start our colony. This would be difficult enough, but that wasn't all. It was necessary that the beaver family be located in a part of the country where there were mink, marten, lynx, etc., as Archie didn't intend to give up the trap-line altogether.

We finally beached our canoe at a campsite a mile from Senneterre. Because it was too close to town for the safety of the Macs, we stopped there only so that Archie could go into town to get the mail and some groceries. Shortly after he left, the two Macs awoke and began to complain about being cooped up in the stove. Through the stove-pipe hole I talked and talked to them in an effort to reassure them. I was busy at this when I heard a voice.

I looked over my shoulder, and there stood a tall, elderly Indian. He said something to me in a language I couldn't understand, so I said, 'I'm sorry, but I don't understand you.' (He had spoken Algonquin.)

'Oh dat's all right. I just want to know what you talking to dat stove for?'

At the sound of the strange voice the beaver had become quiet, so that my conversation with an inanimate object must have made him think I was off my rocker.

'I'm talking to the beaver,' I told him.

He was sure then that I was heading for the laughing academy (mental institution).

It turned out that the Indian, whose name was Dave Whitestone (French name: David Pelon), knew my father. As youths, he and Father had gone logging and had been on many a river-drive together. Speaking to one who knew my father gave me such a feeling of longing that I wanted to go home right there and then. Since the time when I said that I'd never go back, I'd succeeded fairly well in shutting out all thoughts of home and family. I had even ceased to write any more.

I accepted Dave's invitation to tea, and while in his tent I turned the Macs loose. I expected them to make a dash for the lake, but they were content to lie in my lap until Archie returned.

'This is Mr. Whitestone – he knows Papa,' I said to Archie. I choked up and couldn't continue. I made a hurried exit. When I came back again, Archie and Dave were already like two old friends. Archie told us that he had hired out as a guide on a ten-day moose hunt. Dave asked, 'Where is dem sports come from?'

'From Florida, there's eight in the party.'

'Den I think I'll go and get a job dere too,' said Dave, and he left.

When Archie saw how I was feeling, he insisted that I go to see my father immediately. 'Here's your chance,' he urged. 'I'll be gone for ten days, and if you take the next train you'll have a good week's visit. If you'd like to stay a little longer – well, what's a couple of days?'

'What about the beaver? I can't take them on a train.'

'Dammit then, I'll take you home myself in the canoe – beaver and all!'

This was possible, as we could have stepped into the canoe from where we were sitting and paddled to within a mile of my home. It sounds easy, but it would have taken us at least six weeks to get there.

My trip home didn't materialize, but we did end up in a part of Canada that we never dreamed of, or even knew existed.

Dave arrived from town with a man whom we shall call Joe. Joe was a Micmac Indian, from eastern Quebec and New Brunswick, he said. We had no reason to doubt this, but the balance of what he told us was pure fabrication. Baron Munchausen was a piker compared to Joe!

Joe excelled in everything he put his hand to, according to his own testimony. 'Right now,' he said, 'I'm out of work, because they kicked me out of the carnival – I'm too tough for the ring.' When he discovered we were trappers, he drew in a sharp breath and went on. 'Oh hell, do you call this trapping country? Well, it ain't. You should go into the Touladi country, dere's where your fur is! Why, one night I was attacked by a lynx when I went to the lake for water.'

'Where is this Touladi you speak of?' Archie enquired.

'It's on the line between Quebec and New Brunswick.'

Before he had a chance to blast off again, Archie asked, 'Are there any beaver there?'

'Beaver, did'ja say? Why they're just thick,' said Joe, peering through his closely grouped fingers, 'and there's even a kind of land beaver. ...' On and on he rambled with glowing tales of his Touladi country, his hunting-lodge, his boat – a yacht, really. He was, bar none, the most entertaining liar that any of us had ever heard. When he finally left, Dave picked up a pinch of sand and said, 'Even if dis much is true – it would be a hell of a good place to go.' Archie agreed. In retrospect, it is incomprehensible that a man like Joe should influence, in any way, men like Archie and Dave, but he did.

Archie and I set off for the Touladi in the fall of 1928, with Dave to follow later. I'd never questioned Archie's decisions on serious matters, so I guess I just went along for the ride, and, with the beaver, what a ride it turned out to be. At one point a sympathetic train conductor permitted us to free the beaver in the coach. We completed the trip in the baggage car, because of the impossibility of bringing poplar branches and basins of water into the coach.

We detrained at Cabano, Quebec, about forty or fifty miles west of the New Brunswick border. While we waited to unload our canoe and packs, I kept busy looking after the frisky beaver. Archie just looked busily grim. I put this down to the possibility that he was train-sick. He hadn't told me that our bank-roll consisted of less than three dollars.

Archie had trapped in three very poor hunting-grounds in a row. The Sunset Lodge winter was one of the worst, financially. That year he'd been caught by freeze-up and forced to take what available territory there was. (He'd lost valuable time coming to my house to visit me.)

That year he'd also been laid up with strychnine poisoning, had built Pony Hall, and had made two extra trips to Forsythe on my account. A wasted winter, really. From then on it seemed impossible for him to save enough money to put aside for a rainy day.

Taking advantage of a quiet moment, I shut the beaver into their crates and looked around to size up Cabano. From the station platform it appeared to be a neat, clean town. A stone church stood tall amidst the little, frame houses. Trees lined the wooden sidewalk. In the distance I sighted a lake and a well-timbered mountain. On the opposite shore of the lake, in fact, there appeared to be an endless forest. At least, I thought to myself, that part of Joe's story was true.

Archie interrupted my observations, saying, 'I've arranged for a wagon to take our things down to the wharf.' (There were still many horse-drawn vehicles in that town.)

We set off for the lake. The old horse plugged along, pulling the wagon over the bumpy road. Archie and I took the board-walk.

When they first saw us, the few citizens who were about that early morning either wheeled around and ran the other way, or just stood agog in their tracks. Some stepped off the street to let us by. Their strange behaviour was scarcely to be blamed. It isn't every day that one sees a couple of befringed, buck-skin-clad figures perambulating up the street. More astonishing still was Archie, with his long hair, packing a stove full of beaver on his back. The cry of the young beaver sounds much like the wail of an infant, so they naturally assumed that this was our way of transporting our babies.

Some hope revived in us as we stood on the shore of beautiful Temiscouata Lake. The flaming colours of autumn ranged as far as we could see on the opposite shore, a solid forest afire in autumn splendour.

Archie said, 'It's possible that they don't kill off all the animals here as we do up north, so perhaps, maybe, we stand a chance of starting a beaver colony on the Touladi after all. I'm not foolish enough to expect to make a big hunt. I'll be satisfied if we only make ends meet. Is that O.K. with you?'

It was. Come to think of it, we'd never done much else. Not that I thought of it then, but I wasn't losing a thing by going into the conservation business. I was much too happy over the change in Archie's attitude towards trapping to worry about where our next bannock was coming from.

Archie pointed towards the east. 'We'll head towards that dip – I think there's an inlet there.'

'Oh come on, I'm hungry,' I said.

'O.K., let's go.'

We pushed off and threw the troll out. Luckily, we caught a huge jackfish. Archie was right; there was an inlet exactly where he had indicated. It was a dandy creek, just right for the beaver. We made camp in the lovely elm grove by the brook, and while Archie was setting up the tent, I cleaned the fish and made a fried bannock. We were so busy getting wood, water, and boughs for bedding and flooring in the tent, both of us tired and hungry, that we didn't notice that Mac and Mac were not running about getting underfoot as was usual when we made camp.

When we finally investigated, we found them scratching violently at themselves. They moaned pitifully as they scratched until they bled. Their small bodies were covered with a rash. We took them to a doctor, who advised us not to feed them any more bread or porridge – or chocolates, which we had treated them to on the train – as these foods overheated their blood. He suggested we give them Pablum if the Macs refused their natural food, such as leaves and bark. He also gave us a tin of ointment for the rash. When Archie explained apologetically about our lack of funds, this kind man said, 'Never mind. Come again when you need me.'

We stopped at a nearby store to buy the Pablum. The grocer wrapped it, saying, 'That will be seventy-five cents.' We didn't have it, so Archie asked, 'Will you charge it?'

'Why yes, monsieur. Anything else?' As Archie put it in *Pilgrims of the Wild*: 'I crossed my fingers, touched wood, changed feet and could have used some prayers if I'd had any. He was asking for it, so I took the bull by the horns. . . .' We walked out of there owing well over one hundred dollars. We had our winter's provisions, or almost.

We'd no sooner returned to our camp and rubbed the beaver with the ointment, than a group of people came. They were a jolly crowd, most interested in the Macs, who had quieted down after their rub-down. The ladies immediately fell in love with them. The men, on hearing our plans, were more concerned for our welfare. They informed us that the Touladi country had been heavily 'cut' and there was nothing there but slash.

Archie looked sick – this was bad news. They also told us that we'd find a lake, Birch Lake, at the head of the Horton branch, a river that flowed into the Touladi, where the lumbermen had not yet reached. This, then, was where we would go.

We had to hire a truck to take us forty miles to a settlement of habitants called Squatec, and there, at last, we came to the Touladi River. We launched the canoe and paddled and poled for mile upon mile through the devastated country. Even when we reached the Horton branch, there was still no end in sight to the ravaged, timberless land.

We began to doubt that Birch Lake had escaped the axe. There was, even now, snow on the ground and ice forming on our paddles or poles, whichever we were using, as we pushed our way upriver; so we couldn't afford to go farther on. We made camp at the Horton, and Archie went exploring for the lake. He followed an old, overgrown tote road through muskeg and cedar swamps. The going was terrible, he told me on his return, but the slash ended on this side of the lake, and the rest was untouched.

I was elated to hear this, but not too happy when he told me that we had to go six miles overland. There was nothing for it but to start packing. What a blood-sweating portage that was! By the time we got around to felling trees for our cabin, winter had closed in. We worked until we thought we'd drop, chopping down trees, hauling the logs to the building-site, and chopping the frozen moss out from beneath the snow for chinking.

One night, after a particularly exhausting day, I sat propped against the bed-roll, weary and discouraged. I was sure that the cabin would never, never materialize. I was so down that I even rebelled at having to make the daily bannock. Archie, who had come to recognize that look, said, 'Hey, I'll make the bannock if you'll throw a stitch in this.' He threw me a sock with a hole in it big enough to drive a herd of caribou through.

'I suppose a change is as good as a rest,' I sighed.

'What's the matter, kid? Cheer up! You'll be moving into your new home tomorrow,' he announced brightly.

This was the best news yet. 'In that case, let's celebrate,' I said.

Archie went along with the joke. 'Yeah, let's. I'll make a great big bannock.' With a flourish he heaped the bowl with flour, added salt, and rummaged in the grub-box for the baking powder. While his back was turned, McGinty, the opportunist, spied the abandoned bowl. She came at a dead gallop, zoomed through the air, and landed plop in the middle, sending flour in all directions.

Archie's shocked surprise convulsed me, but I didn't dare laugh, because it was an awful thing for McGinty to have done.

Then a wild and noisy battle erupted. Archie shouted her name and mine alternately as he tried desperately to pull her away, but McGinty had a firm grip on the bowl and was determined to stay. Archie was at his wit's end, for it was like fighting a whirring electric fan in a tub of feathers. The overwhelming speed with which Mac propelled her webbed hind feet through the flour forced Archie to let her down.

The atmosphere was so thick with flour that I could barely see them. The scuffle ended at last in victory for Archie, and McGinty ambled off in a huff. She was not in the least repentant. She cast malignant glances at Archie as she sat back, cleaning her flour-clogged nostrils with clenched fists. Such was the stand the beaver invariably took to preserve their rights.

McGinty's personal celebration over moving into our new cabin was a little premature, as the chinking still had to be done, and, owing to the frozen timber we'd used to build it, it would be an ice-house until the wood thawed – a week at least. If we hadn't been so particular in our choice of building-site, we could have completed our home in half the time. To avoid the sight of stumps and slash we cut the logs quite a distance back, but it was well worth the effort.

We were settled in a magnificent grove of birch and pine. When the chintz curtains had been hung, and cupboard, table, and stands decked out with new oilcloth coverings, and the shining deerskin rugs laid, one couldn't have wished for a more cozy nest in which to live.

Our proud Birch Lake cabin. As we struggled and slaved in its construction, little did we know that it would one day be known the world over as the 'House of McGinnis', and that it would also be the inspiration for Archie's *Tales of an Empty Cabin*. It was pure luck that there happened to be a live beaver-house on the lake. So now we had a home and a start on the beaver colony.

We were happy and content, the Macs and I, but I could see this wasn't so with Archie. When he wasn't alert to my scrutiny, I could tell that he was desperately worried and depressed. Being impractical, I couldn't understand why the shroud. His anxieties were well founded, however, for our provisions weren't going to last forever – eight weeks if we were careful. After that, what? So far we'd seen scarcely a sign of fur-bearing animals, and we still had a store bill to pay. Obviously there would be no trapping, and the only jobs available for men in the vicinity were those of lumberjack, sawmill-worker, or farm-hand – all jobs that Archie loathed. He hated with a burning hatred to see the forests go under the axe and the land under the plough.

Once we'd moved into our home, Archie wasted no time in brooding about the future. He was off with his trapping equipment the next day. After he left, I once more bitterly wondered if we would ever leave this cruel way of earning a livelihood. I had the same sinking feeling that had made my last months on the Marque so miserable. To lighten my mood, I slipped into my snowshoe bridles and hiked the three or four miles down the portage to where we had a cache.

We had been so pressed for time on our way to Birch Lake that we had left a fifty-pound box of books and magazines there. There were also two sacks of potatoes and one of onions, both frozen solid – that was the reason for leaving them in the first place. I'd heard somewhere that frozen vegetables become edible if put in boiling water to cook. I decided to try it and put a couple of pounds in the pack-sack on top of the books, where they rattled like rocks all the way home. My hearsay information proved correct – the vegetables cooked up fine.

Late one night, a week following Archie's departure, I heard someone at the door. I felt it couldn't be Archie because I hadn't heard his usual home-coming call. Who could it be? Mac and Mac scurried into their den, and a cold chill raced up my spine. Then the door swung open, and there was Archie, looking grim as death.

'For God's sake, what happened to you?' I cried, running to him.

He put his arms around me. 'Poor "Ting", always worrying. I'm O.K. But how is everything here?' He tried to look cheerful, but I could see discouragement written all over him. 'Oh hell,' he said, as he went to the bunk to remove his moccasins, 'there isn't a damn thing in this country – a few mink, perhaps, but not half enough to pay our bill.'

Not knowing what to say, I went on preparing supper for him.

'Oh, there's a fox out there,' he began.

'Did you set for him?' I interrupted, hoping that he hadn't.

'No, what's the use. He'd just be a drop in the bucket, and I imagine that his life would mean more to him than that. After all, it's the only one he's got.' He laughed, mirthlessly.

Mac and Mac came charging at a gallop to make a big fuss over Archie. It was impossible to resist these jolly roly-polies, and we all had a playful suppertime together.

After the Macs went to work in their den, Archie insisted on sitting before the open stove, instead of going to bed for a much-needed rest. He gazed into the fire, eyes smouldering, hotter than the burning coals.

'Look, Archie,' I said, 'we have everything – really everything that one could wish, so why are you so worried and sad?'

'Me sad? No. I'm not sad,' he said, giving me that penetrating look. 'I'm just mad. Crazier than ol' hell. A leopard can't change his spots you know. When he does, he's dead. Like me. Why I wouldn't give five cents for a man like me. Take it easy, kid,' he said, seeing how this nonsensical outburst alarmed me. 'I was only thinking of the spaniel that my aunt had.'

'Oh, tell me about the spaniel,' I said, pretending that I believed him.

'My aunt, as you know, was a great one for training people and things, like a little dog. Do you know what that cruel bitch used to do?'

'Archie!' I exclaimed.

'Well, anyway, she had three rags, white, red, and blue. She'd drop these on the lawn and tell the dog to bring back the colour that she had demanded of him. It was all guess-work for the dog, of course, and so back and forth he'd go, for hours on end. When he did accidentally bring the right colour, she'd let him know by patting him briskly a couple of times on the head. Then she'd go and switch the colours around. Naturally, at her next command he'd run to where he'd scored that last time, but he'd be wrong again; and on and on it went. I know exactly how that poor dog felt, and so I should because I went through the same thing myself! I've read since then,' he continued, 'that dogs are colour-blind – so-o-o she wasn't as smart as she thought she was.' He lapsed into a gloomy silence and then broke it with a heavy sigh. 'I'll have to get those beaver down the lake.'

'Archie, don't you dare!'

He was talking of the beaver family that we meant to start our colony with! We quarrelled long and hard, till at last he burst out, 'All right then, I'll just sit here like a bum and let us all starve.'

In the morning he picked up his traps and turned towards the lake.

'Wait for me, I'm coming with you,' I said.

I didn't know how I would stop him from trapping our beaver, but it had to be done and that was all there was to it.

As he prepared the traps I climbed to the top of the beaver-house and cocked my head as if I heard something.

'Listen Archie, they sound just like Mac and Mac,' I lied.

'Don't be silly,' he snapped.

'But the kittens are fighting over something. They *do* sound exactly like Mac and Mac,' I insisted.

He set the last trap and came forward. 'Let's go,' he said gruffly.

Just then the water heaved in an opening in the ice, indicating that a beaver had left the house. It would be the mother beaver coming out to ward off any threat to her family. Would she get into one of the traps?

Without a word Archie dashed over and sprang all the sets, rendering them harmless. That was the last time he ever set a trap – that is, for money.

He was glum and irritable for several days. Finally he blurted 'I never, never, thought that I would see the day when I would come to this.'

'Stop it right now, Archie,' I yelled. 'I'm sick and tired of your moping.'

'I'm sorry, Gurdy, but the only thing that I can do for you is to save up a couple of pension cheques and buy you a ticket home. I have nothing, not anything, to offer you.'

'O.K., if that's the way you want it. Ever since you quit the infernal trap-line you've been thinking you're finished.' Then he came to me and apologized.

Since he'd reached his lowest ebb, he couldn't possibly go anywhere but up, and he began taking an interest in things, and started to do a lot of reading. At night, to save coal oil, we'd sit in front of the open stove, or look through the window if there was a moon, and he'd talk of the old Bisco days, of Big Otter, Gitchimeguin, Alex Espaniol, and Ne-ganikabo (Stands First). He told me many, many stories, some of them fictitious, but most of them true.

One night I asked him, 'Why not write them down so we'll be able to read them together when we get old and grey?'

'I feel as old and grey as I'll ever feel. Besides, I'll never forget the old days, so why bother writing?'

There happened to be an article in one of the magazines that suggested that the Forestry Branch drop strychnine pellets from airplanes to destroy the wolves in Algonquin Park in Ontario. Archie read it, and this ridiculous, dangerous idea so infuriated him that he wrote down his opinion of it on the margin of the story. Soon he ran out of space and found some sheets of paper and continued. Before he finished, he had written thirty pages.

From then on he began to jot down ideas. Soon he was taking his scribbling more seriously, and if a sentence didn't come up to par, he would work at it till it did.

During this period he found another pastime. He began to make an Indian war-bonnet from the feathers of an owl that had been caught in a fox-set when we were in the Jumping Caribou country. When the headpiece was finished, he carved an Indian head from a block of wood and painted the friendship sign on its face. When the war-bonnet was placed upon it, it really was quite impressive.

It was fun having Archie back to normal again; he even remembered that Christmas was only two weeks off and said that he would have to go to the settlement to get a few things. This was good news to me – it gave me the chance to say what had been in the back of my mind since he had started writing. I gave him the stack of pages that he'd written, for by now he had mounds of material, and said, in an offhand manner, 'Hey honey, get busy and parcel this up, because we'll have to send them to one of those magazines.'

'What! Have you gone out of your mind?' he asked in astonishment.

'No, but if you don't send them, I will', I threatened.

However, after a lot of argument and coaxing he finally said, 'Yes – why not? They can only shoot me.'

Of course he had to rewrite the stuff, but after it was finished, how daring we felt as we went through the magazines trying to figure the best one to send his article to. The final choice was *Country Life,* an English publication.

The very next morning he started on the journey to the settlement. Before leaving, he said, 'I'm going to make this a Christmas to end all Christmases; after all, it might be our last.'

He was pessimistic, but cheerful.

At breakfast I'd handed him a sealed envelope. It contained a list of two items. These were my Christmas gifts to him. Nothing splashy, unless one could term a suit of long woolen underwear as such. Still, if they turned out to be red . . . . The other item was a large, black silk handkerchief, which he always wore in winter instead of a cap of any kind.

Where would we get the money for the celebration? There would be two of Archie's war pension cheques waiting in the post office at the settlement.

He returned, true to his word, on Christmas Eve. My, how glad we were, the two Macs and I, when he burst in hauling the toboggan, load and all, into the cabin! After a hug from me and a frolicsome welcome from Mac and Mac, Archie began to unload the toboggan. He'd brought things that he didn't want them to see until later, so he gave them each a candy stick, and while they were distracted with these he showed me the toys he'd bought them.

There was a clown on wheels that made a noisy clack-clack when pulled by its long orange-coloured handle, a bunny with a tinkly bell, also on wheels, and, to my surprise and delight, he'd also bought yards and yards of red and white crepe-paper streamers, a Chinese lantern for the ceiling, and red, green, and silver baubles for the window. I could hardly wait to start the festivities, so as soon as I'd whipped up a quick meal for Archie, I lost no time in getting at the decorations.

Trying to balance myself while standing on a block of wood on a pole floor, with a mouthful of tacks, streamers in one hand and hammer in the other, was no small feat. With Archie's helpful suggestions, the Christmas trimming was soon complete. By this time I'd become so immersed in the spirit of Christmas,

I simply had to go and get a tree for the beaver. Archie laughed, but I paid no attention and went on out into the night, heading towards the woods as fast as my snowshoes could carry me. The blizzard that had been blowing earlier had run its course, and except for a few racing clouds it was a beautiful night.

But I couldn't spare the time for star-gazing, since, like any 'parent', I was intent on giving the Macs the best Christmas ever.

With a perfect balsam slung over my shoulder, I went joyfully homeward, but when I entered the shadows of the black spruce, memories of Christmas at home came flooding over me, and without knowing it, I said, 'Oh, Papa!' Startled by my own voice, I stopped and stood still, and there in the darkness I imagined my father sitting in his old rocker, listening to Grandma playing Christmas music on the organ as she used to do, by our candle-lit tree.

I believed I could hear her, while at the same time the bells of our church were ringing. The bells and the organ were mixed up like my emotions. I wasn't sure whether I was sad or glad. Just as a wave of longing swept over me, Archie appeared. He'd worried about my long absence and had come to see if I was all right.

'Oh – here you are!' he said, coming forward and kissing me. A kiss when both parties are on snowshoes leaves much to be desired. Try it sometime.

Archie hadn't been idle while I was out, for he'd hung the Chinese lantern, and on the table were dishes heaped with apples, oranges, chocolates, candies, and nuts. A dazzling sight for one who hadn't seen anything like it in months. I had no time for gorging – my mind was still busy with the Christmas tree.

The usual trimmings would have been harmful to the beaver, so we loaded their tree with apples cut in sections, seeded prunes, pieces of bannock, chocolate, long reeds of macaroni, nuts, and candy sticks. We placed our supper on the table and sat back to watch what the Macs would do when they first discovered Santa had come.

McGinty was the first to spot this windfall. She stood and sniffed cautiously, then sampled a piece of chocolate and went completely haywire. Greedily she tried to take everything all at once. Then, what she least desired happened. McGinnis arrived on the scene. She planted herself solidly between him and the tree, but McGinnis, out to get his share of the goodies, gave her a push that sent her sprawling. McGinnis plucked a big, fat prune from the tree just as McGinty came bounding back. With a quick flip of her short little arm, she whisked the prune from his grasp, and it sailed across the floor.

Caught unaware, McGinnis looked positively comical. While he stood there considering what had happened, McGinty ran after the prune, but before she could pop it all into her mouth, McGinnis made a flying tackle, sending them both tumbling. They scrambled to an upright position and the battle was on. McGinty, with the prune still clamped in her mouth, tried desperately to free herself, but McGinnis held tight and forced her backwards. McGinty found a firm toe-hold and pushed him away. Back and forth they went until it looked like some sort of dance. Then, suddenly, as if by some signal, they raced together for the tree.

We turned to our supper of potatoes, a saddle of venison and gravy, and 'store-bought' pudding.

When gift time came, we gave the now-stuffed beaver their toys, and while they examined them closely, I handed Archie his presents, still wrapped in store paper. It wasn't till he began ripping the parcel open, that I worried over the clerk's choice. I needn't have, for there they were – the glamorous underwear – and they *were* red!

New Year's Eve, minus the toots, whistles, champagne, and laughter, found Archie and me sitting before the open stove, quietly trying to work out a plan for our beaver colony. Breaking a long silence, Archie said, 'You've seen on the way in how the bush has been slashed to the hilt. I'd say that there's about forty square miles of it. That's a lot of territory. That part of the country will be out of commission for commercial use for years, and most animals and men will go out of their way to avoid a slash, so it'll be a safe place for our colony. At least for a while.'

'But if there aren't any trees, what will the beaver use for food?'

'Don't have to worry about that. By the time our beaver

104

overflow into that area, there'll be plenty of food for them. Poplar grow like weeds, you know.'

'Oh, good. Archie, how many beaver do you think there are in that house on the lake?'

'Six, at least.'

'Hurray! Then counting Mac and Mac, we have eight beaver. That's a good start if ever there was one.'

Archie, not so optimistic, interrupted 'Don't kid yourself, it's going to be a long haul. First of all, if we are to protect the beaver, we'll have to stay with them for six months of the year – from the end of November to the last of May. So that gives me exactly six months to earn the winter's grub, clothing, etc.'

This took some of the wind out of my sails. I thought for a moment, then suggested that I stay and look after the Macs while he was at work and asked where he thought he could get a job.

'Oh, I guess I can get work in one of those sawmills.'

'But you can't! You know how you hate . . . '

He waved me to silence and continued. 'I'll work in the mill till the hunting season is open and then go guiding. When the guiding season is over, it'll be high time for us to be getting back here to the beaver.'

Birch Lake is where we intended to start our colony. I was to spend the summer with the Macs at the same spot we camped at when we first came to Lake Temiscouata. Those were the plans.

March came in like a lion, so we had to wait till it blew itself out before going to the settlement for such things as coal oil, matches, and groceries. When the weather had turned nice and mild, we knew that the Macs would be in no danger if left for two or three nights. Mild weather means heavy snow-shoeing by day, so we travelled at night. How exhilarating it was to be on the trail again. I hadn't realized how much I'd missed it.

We arrived at the store (the store and post office were in the same shop) about noon. Since neither of us ever wrote to any-one, our only reason for going to the post office was to pick up those ever-blessed pension cheques. You can imagine our surprise when Archie was handed a large important-looking envelope and a magazine, securely tied. Archie examined the envelope carefully, turning it over and surveying it from all possible angles.

'Oh, for heaven sakes, open it up,' I cried impatiently, as I tried unsuccessfully to get at the magazine.

'It's from England,' said Archie, mystified. He slit the envelope open with his hunting-knife and pulled out a letter. In its folds, lo and behold, was a pretty, pink cheque! *Country Life* had accepted Archie's article, but that wasn't all. They were asking for more. This is when Archie gave 'with the war-whoop'.

'Is something wrong?' asked the storekeeper apprehensively.

'Not at all, in fact, quite the contrary,' said Archie, grinning as he waved the cheque. By this time I'd ripped the wrapper off the magazine and found the article that Archie had written. I ran to the storekeeper and, pointing at the page, said, 'Look at that, my husband wrote that all by himself!' How proud I was. He looked at the pictures and read here and there, then said, 'Say, maybe you've got something there.' I could tell that he was more than surprised that an odd-looking character like Archie could even read, let alone write.

We bought a few things for ourselves and a lot of treats for the Macs. Then Archie signed his two pension cheques in the usual way, but when it came to the one from *Country Life*, he cleared his throat and signed it with an elegant flourish. What an actor! We laughed, especially the storekeeper.

I was jubilant. 'Just think, Archie, now you can write about all kinds of things, and that means that we can both stay with the beaver.'

'Not so fast, kid. I doubt very much that I can keep it up.' I didn't doubt that Archie could write.

The mild weather had turned to rain, which made snow-shoeing impossible, so we were at the village for two and a half days before it turned cold enough to travel. This meant that by the time we were able to start the return trip home, Mac and Mac had been three nights alone. We had no intention of leaving them for so long, and we were worried. We left the village before daylight and it was long after dark when we came to our lake. Just before leaving the woods Archie cut some

A father beaver builds the lodge while the young one swims,
centre foreground.

Grey Owl, Anahareo and visitors look at trees felled by beaver.

Archie and Dawn, probably 1935. His costume was made by Anahareo and took five moosehides and about two pounds of beads.

Grey Owl uses his moose call.

Grey Owl in buckskin dress
probably made by Anahareo.

Anahareo holds a beaver kitten.

Anahareo in 1934.

With a whiskey jack in winter.

Dawn, aged seven years, at left,
with Jelly Roll and friend.

Anahareo holds a
sturgeon.

poplar saplings with the idea of shoving them under the ice for the wild beaver, a small gift considering that they were the very foundation of our mission in life.

When we got up to the beaver-house, Archie said, 'Something's wrong.' He lit a match, and there we saw fresh snowshoe tracks! My first thought was that someone who had known of the existence of the family of beaver had taken advantage of our absence and had come and trapped them. Then it struck me that McGinty and McGinnis might have been killed too. I panicked.

We left the toboggan behind and sped the rest of the way to the cabin. Archie pushed the door open, and coming towards us with outstretched hand was old Dave. Limp with relief and delighted to see him, we soon had the toboggan inside the shack and were chuckling over Mac and Mac, who were having a whale of a time 'helping' to unload it. It was a pleasure to buy things for them, because their gratitude and enjoyment were so obvious. The cabin was filled with joyous excitement, all of us happy to be together and everyone talking at the same time – even the beaver had much to say. Old Dave sat, smiling whimsically, as we endeavoured to bring the camp to order.

When our emotions subsided and an elaborate supper was well on the way, Dave went to the wash-stand and, from behind the water-pail, brought forth a huge, black bundle. Smiling, he handed it to Archie.

'See,' he said, 'I thought I might as well make myself useful while I was here.'

The lamp glow reflected the gleaming wet fur of a freshly skinned beaver!

I was dumbfounded, and poor Archie, in a strained voice, tried to thank old Dave, who, sensing something was wrong, was watching us uncomfortably. Whatever was said to get over that painful moment does not matter. Dave had killed all the beaver on the lake, believing he was doing us a good turn. His deed, instead, had destroyed the very ground-work of our plans.

Archie and I left that part of the country as early as possible in the spring of '29, since we had no reason to remain. We located a small lake between Squatec and Cabano, about thirty miles north-east of Cabano and moved to it. The two Macs immediately went exploring while we stayed in camp and performed the usual chores of making camp. After a short time they returned. They had come in quest of bannock, which they ate noisily in their rush to get back to the lake.

They coaxed us to go with them, but we were too busy making camp, and they left without us. We regretted this many times afterwards, because that was the last time we were to see them.

It is a beaver's nature to leave home to roam in the spring, but the year-old kittens return after they have had their fling. Archie and I were much too distressed to sit and wait for them. We raced over the country in a frantic but fruitless search. They had no fear of man and could be clubbed to death without difficulty. We followed creek after creek until they had all petered out and disappeared into the swamps.

One day, Archie leaned against a tree to relieve his foot, which had begun to ache. Rain, discouragement, and disappointment etched his face.

'I'm afraid this is it. We've had the works,' he said.

'What do you mean?'

Waving his arm with finality he indicated the creek. 'This is the end of this creek and the last of them all. There's no more places to look. It's the end of Mac and Mac. And take a look at this foot.'

I rushed to him and looked. His foot was so swollen that the moccasin was stretched to the breaking-point. I stooped to undo it, but Archie brushed me away.

'No, no, we daren't take it off; if we do we'll never get it back on again. We'd better get back to camp.'

Dave had just come in from his hunting-ground and was waiting for us when we arrived. He took one look at Archie's face and cried, 'What's the matter, chum, are you shot?' He repeated the question as he ran to Archie.

'No Dave, it's that damn foot. It's giving me hell again.'

Dave helped Archie into the tent, and we both worked at untying the moccasins. 'Boy oh boy,' said Dave when he examined the swollen foot. He ordered me to get some hot water to soak the foot. 'No, that's what's wrong with it, Dave,' said Archie. 'It's had too much water.' 'Yeah,' said Dave, 'but it was icy water.' And so it was, for it was early spring. We eased Archie's foot into the pail, which gave him some relief.

After supper Archie said, 'Well, old-timer, how did the spring hunt come out?'

'I guess I can't kick. I got two lynx, a couple of otter, mink, and I guess all the beaver in the country.' Archie and I glanced at each other.

'No, come to think of it, there's one beaver-house I didn't touch.'

'How come?' asked Archie.

'I figured that by the time I could get to them, there'd be young ones in the house.'

'I can't imagine that would stop you,' said Archie sardonically.

'Whaaa – I guess I thought about your two beavers.'

Archie changed the subject by asking Dave what plans he had made for the summer.

'I'd like to go up to that gold I found in Opemiska [Chibougamau country], but I won't have enough money.'

'That pack of furs should get you there,' said Archie nodding towards a pack-sack.

'Not with the fur prices down so low. I have to buy a canoe too – the one I'm using belongs to another fella. What are you two going to do?'

'I don't know,' Archie said hesitantly. 'Trapping was my living, but since I quit . . . '

'Oh, you'll get over it,' Dave assured him.

'Not a chance. I'll work in a sawmill if I have to.'

'Ha, ha,' laughed Dave. 'I can just see you doing that.'

'I'll have to do something – guiding, maybe. I hear there's a resort – Metis Beach, wherever that is.'

'But what about Mac and Mac?' I cried. 'They might come back.' There was a long pause.

At last Archie spoke. 'I'm sorry, but I don't think there's a chance of that. We've hunted every possible place. They're gone. Either shot or trapped.'

A full month later, June, Archie still couldn't bear putting any weight on his foot, and our financial worries mounted by the day. Since we couldn't pay our bill, we couldn't ask for more credit at the store for groceries. Archie and I sat by the fire, trying to find a solution to our problems. At last Archie said, 'I'm sorry I got you into this, kid.'

'Into what?' I asked.

'You know, don't you, that I can see no further than my next pension cheque. Me and my big ideas. Trying to save the beaver from extinction, and here I am, not even able to save those we had. I can't save you, me – nothing. I must have been crazy.'

'Maybe we can't do it right now, but we'll find a way, just wait and see.' I looked at his foot and added, 'Just don't worry any more.'

'Don't worry?' he cried. 'I have never in my life been in such a spot – a dead-end. I'm going to town tomorrow and try to get a job.'

He forced himself to take a step, then another, but he doubled up in pain. 'I can't make it, I can't walk,' he groaned, and sat down, head in hands. I was trying to comfort him when Dave arrived.

'Dave, where in heck have you been all day?' I asked. He dropped his pack beside me, saying, 'Here is some meat. The bush is just thick with deer.'

Hoping to take Archie out of his mood of despair, I sprang up and said, 'Oh boy, let's cook it up right now with some fried bannock.' Dave nodded in agreement and said, 'That sounds good to me. The way I feel right now I could eat the left hind-leg of a horse and ask for more.' Then turning to Archie, Dave asked, 'What's the matter? The foot worse?'

'No, but I still can't walk.' The two men began to talk and I prepared the meat for cooking and mixed the bannock.

Then, I heard Archie say, 'Dave, old boy, you'd better pull out of here, before your money is all gone. I know what you're up to. You don't want to leave us in this shape. I appreciate it, believe me, but I want to make sure that you get back to a country where you know how to make a living. I want you to head back there tomorrow.'

'But I've got a job coming up. Oh, but before I go how would you like to have another pair of young beaver?'

'Oh yes, *please*,' I cried. 'Where are they?'

'In the house I didn't touch.'

'Thanks, Dave,' Archie said, 'but I don't think we ought to get another pair. We might lose them the same way we did Mac and Mac.'

'Ah, they'll be killed by this time next year anyway,' said Dave.

'What you say is only too true. But I can't go for them with this,' Archie responded gloomily, pointing to his foot swollen almost twice its normal size.

Because of the condition of his foot, Archie was unable to accompany Dave to Sugar Loaf Mountain where we were to get the beaver. I went along instead. In a week we returned with two kitten beaver. One we named after the mountain from which he came, Sugar Loaf. The other we named Jelly Roll. The villainous jinx that had urged Dave to trap our beaver that day in March was still dogging our trail. Not being satisfied with this first outrage, nor with the subsequent loss of McGinnis and McGinty, it also took little Sugar Loaf. This pitiful creature died less than three weeks after we got him.

Disheartening as all this was, it did not prevent Archie from carrying out our original ideas. Through these past misfortunes we learned that the cards were so resolutely stacked against the beaver that even we, who had only their welfare at heart, had caused them as much grief as had their deadliest enemies. And this realization fired Archie's determination more than ever to see that they got a better deal.

If Dave hadn't helped us we would have been hard put for food. When Archie's foot healed, he decided that we should go to Metis Beach, a resort on the south shore of the St. Lawrence River, in the hope that he might find a job, guiding.

There we were worse off than ever, as no jobs were available for him. One day, I saw a 'Maid wanted, Scandinavian' notice in the post office, and without telling Archie, I decked myself out in my boots, breeches, and buckskin shirt and went to the address. A large, blonde woman answered my knock, with an enquiring 'Ja?'

'I saw your notice in the post office, and I w-want a j-j-job,' I stuttered.

The lady smiled, but said nothing. Then a tall dark-haired woman appeared in the hallway and as she approached, she beckoned me inside. 'I'm Mrs. Peck. I'm sorry, but that notice in the post office means that I merely want someone else's Scandinavian maid to come and visit with mine. She is lonely here, for we don't speak her language.'

I rose to go, and noting my discouragement she added, 'Do sit down, please. I've seen you and your husband passing by and wondered – what does he do?'

'He's a guide. We came here hoping that he would find a job.'

'But this is not that kind of resort. There is no fishing or hunting here.' Then impatiently, she asked, 'Can't he support you? Have you any money?'

'Yes,' I replied indignantly, 'he has always supported me. He doesn't know that I'm here. No, we have no money at all. The last we had was from an article he wrote for a magazine and that's all gone now.'

'Who published the article,' asked Mrs. Peck with great interest.

'An English magazine called *Country Life.*'

'How interesting,' she exclaimed.

Warming to the subject, I went on, 'He has a roll of paper with things written in it over at the camp.'

' I wonder if you could bring it to me?' she asked.

'Why do you want it?'

'I'd like to see how and what he writes. I might be able to . . . Yes. Bring it as soon as you can, will you?'

'I'd have to get it without his knowing.'

'Just get it – no matter how – but get it.'

I did. Mrs. Peck read it with mounting interest. She reached for the phone and called her mother. 'What are you doing?' she asked. 'Whatever it is, drop it and come right over. Yes. Right away.'

The two women read excerpts from Archie's notes, exclaiming, 'Marvellous, extraordinary – unique!'

'Your husband has talent,' Mrs. Peck told me, 'there's no doubt about it. My mother and I think the material would be ideal for a lecture. A talk on the wilderness. The people here would love it.'

Wondering what Archie would have to say about this, I asked in a very small voice, 'A lecture?'

'Yes,' she said, 'exactly. Do you think he would do it?'

'I don't know. He's never done it before. He doesn't even know yet that I took that.' I pointed at the manuscript. 'And I dread the thought of telling him.'

'Well, we must,' Mrs. Peck said firmly. 'That's all there is to it. I'll get him even if I have to drag him out.'

'Yes! You do that!' I said with relief.

'I'll be there this evening,' said Mrs. Peck.

Walking back to camp I didn't much relish the ordeal of informing Archie of my clandestine activities. Putting up a brave front, I walked straight into his arms, kissed him, and sat down beside him.

His first words were 'Well, I've got a job. At least we'll eat.'

I sat upright, somewhat deflated. 'What doing? Guiding?'

'In a place like this?' he jeered. 'Of course not.' He pointed to himself. 'Meet the distinguished helper of a gardener.'

'Hmmm,' I murmured, 'I almost got a job today too.'

'What!' he exclaimed. 'So that's what you were up to. Why didn't you tell me you were looking for a job?'

'Because you wouldn't have let me if I had.'

'What kind of logic is that?' he laughed. 'What sort of a job?'

'As a maid.'

'You – a maid?' He glared in disbelief.

His expression unnerved me, and I said almost guiltily, 'Yes,' and then sputtered on about how she had specified a Scandinavian maid.

'This is awful – it gets worse all the time.'

'Don't worry,' I said, 'she was very kind – very concerned. She even asked why you couldn't support me and what kind of work you did.'

'And what did you say to that?' Archie began sarcastically.

'I said you were a writer.'

He jumped up. 'A writer! Oh, no!'

'She thinks you can really write,' I said earnestly.

Archie's anger mounted. 'How would she know?'

'Because,' said I hesitantly, 'I took the notes you had in your box and gave them to her to read.'

'What! You did that?'

'Yes. And she's coming to see you tonight.'

'Why?' Archie asked, guardedly.

'She wants you to lecture in some hall.'

He exploded. 'A lecture. Me! What in hell have you got me into now?' He whirled about and left the tent.

Since Mrs. Peck would be arriving in a few hours, I tidied up the tent and grounds about the outdoor fire. The tea-pail was boiling when Archie returned. He embraced me. 'Sorry, kid. I lost my temper. Poor thing, you're having it rough, and I shouldn't have, especially when I know you just wanted to help.'

When Mrs. Peck and her mother arrived, I cast a worried look at Archie. I needn't have, because their smiles and genuine friendliness disarmed him, and his face shone with a brightness I hadn't seen in a long time.

'Has your wife told you?' Mrs. Peck smiled at Archie.

'Yes – but . . .'

'No buts. You just must give us this talk on wildlife. It's beautiful.'

Archie backed away. 'I'm sorry, lady, but you'll never catch me at that. I wouldn't know where to begin, let alone following through. I'd make a fool of myself – a bigger fool than I am.'

'Now you stop this nonsense, Mr. Belaney.' Mrs. Peck advanced upon him purposefully, fishing the manuscript from her purse. 'A person who can write this has a duty to the public. I've always been against the slaughter of animals.'

'But Mrs. Peck,' protested Archie, 'I couldn't even if I wanted to.'

'You have all the material in here.' She held up his manuscript. 'All you have to do is stand up and read it.'

'That sounds easy. Why don't you let someone else read it then. You're welcome to do so.'

'That won't do at all,' Mrs. Peck said earnestly. 'You wrote it – you have the feeling for it. You believe in this, don't you?'

'I certainly do,' Archie replied emphatically.

'You'll be a knock-out in your buckskins.' Mrs. Peck winked at me and then turned and rushed to her car, her mother right behind her.

Archie shook his fists in the air, shouting, 'I can't – I won't – I *won't.*'

Smiling sweetly at him they waved and drove away.

Archie sighed, 'That's the end of that, I hope.'

The next day Archie arrived home from work carrying much-needed groceries. I went to him, and we stood holding each other until Jelly Roll came tramping over our feet, pushing and pulling at our legs, crying loudly, demanding attention. We stopped to pet and make a big fuss over her. 'Hey, give her an apple.' Archie pulled one from the bag.

'Poor Jelly Roll.' I smiled at her eager face. 'She's had no apples for days and days.' We laughed as she clutched it to her.

'What did you do today?' I asked Archie.

'Pushed a wheelbarrow and the lawn-mower all day. Exciting, eh? I got an advance. Three dollars for the day's work. Here is some news, only don't get excited. The fellow I was working with said that there is a fresh-water pond somewhere near here.'

'Oh Archie, wouldn't it be wonderful. . . .'

'It's on the property of a man who owns half the town,' he continued. 'After supper I'm going to go and ask him if we can take Jelly down for a swim. No, I think I'll do it right now.'

'What about supper?'

'It can wait,' he said good-humouredly, preparing to leave.

Just then Mrs. Peck drove up. She approached us, all aflutter and beaming. She carried a huge basket, and before Archie could say a word, she called out, 'Hello, hello. I've brought us a lunch so we can talk while we munch! Isn't that clever?' she added.

I invited her inside the tent, but Archie said, 'Why not sit out here, it's much nicer and less cramped.' I brought her a blanket to sit on. She removed the cloth from the lunch basket and smoothed it out on the blanket. I couldn't think of a thing to say in a situation like this, so I stammered 'How good of you to do this. It's lovely, but you shouldn't have troubled . . . '

Archie broke in, 'Sh, sh, Gertie, don't say another word. I see some man-size sandwiches, and I'm ready for them. I'm a workingman, you know.'

'Really? I'm so glad. Well, aren't you going to join me?'

'That we will,' Archie agreed.

We sat down to roast beef and ham sandwiches, cookies, cake, and fruit. Jelly Roll held the floor. We had to give her cookies and other bits to keep her out of our food. The conversation was mostly about beaver.

'You know, if it weren't for Mac and Mac, I'd still be a

trapper, killing everything that crossed my trail,' Archie told Mrs. Peck after she had listened to our story.

'But how could you know what you were doing before you learned, from them, that animals have feelings much the same as ours?' she asked with sympathy. 'And that is what you should tell them tomorrow night.'

Archie stopped eating. 'Tell *who* tomorrow night?'

'The people who are coming to hear you lecture tomorrow night, remember?' she enquired calmly.

'Yes, I remember, and I also remember saying that I wouldn't do it. I'm not going to – and that's final.'

'When you said that you believed in the things you wrote,' Mrs. Peck rushed on, 'I took it for granted you would do it. This puts me in an uncomfortable fix. I've rented the ball-room at the best hotel in town. Announcements are up, the invitations mailed. There will be a lot of people there. What am I going to do?'

'Archie,' I reproached him, 'if there's going to be a lot of people there, you should go and tell them what we want to do. Remember what we said when we had Mac and Mac?'

He stared at me, but said nothing for a long time. Finally he spoke to Mrs. Peck. 'Did you say that I could read that stuff of mine?'

'Yes, that's all you have to do.'

'O.K., I'll go. I'll touch it up and we'll be there.'

Archie's talk of his beloved wilderness was a success, but at its conclusion he got an attack of nerves. I too was in a state. I don't suppose we'd have been nervous had we not been so undernourished at the time. We were also worried about Jelly Roll, alone at camp. We couldn't get away fast enough, but were held back by Archie's enthusiastic audience.

After several attempts to leave we bolted for the door, determined that nothing would prevent us this time, only to be stopped by Mrs. Peck, carrying what looked like a hat-box and blocking our way. 'I know how you must feel,' she said. 'I think that we are all a bit tense tonight, but it was well worth the effort. You were marvellous.'

'Thank you, Mrs. Peck,' Archie began, 'but we must be going. The beaver . . . '

'Yes, I know that. But what do you want me to do? Would you like me to open a bank account for you?'

Archie looked questioningly at her, then tiredly asked, 'On what, Mrs. Peck? A dime?'

'Oh, how wrong you are, Mr. Belaney; there's more than a dime in here. Look!' She pulled the lid off the box and inside was a huge stack of money.

'What's this?' asked Archie, puzzled.

Her eyes twinkling mischievously, she answered, 'This is what you brought in tonight.'

'Mrs. Peck! You didn't . . . ' Archie spoke out harshly.

'But Mr. Belaney, I thought you'd be pleased,' she said with disappointment.

'My God. What if I'd been a flop?' Archie gasped.

Mrs. Peck had sold over $700 worth of tickets to Archie's lecture. It was fortunate that Archie hadn't known about this beforehand, or he would have been twice as nervous – if that were possible. As we had awaited zero hour backstage, he'd said, 'Do you know, I'd give anything to get the hell out of this.'

Silently, I had agreed with him. I was feeling guilty for getting him into such a jam.

'I feel like a snake that has swallowed an icicle – chilled from one end to the other,' he'd added dolefully.

I had burst into laughter, and hysteria took over. I couldn't stop until Archie moaned 'It's time to go on!'

Following the initial lecture, Archie was invited to speak at parties, in other halls, and in other hotels. One day a scout-master asked Archie if he would give his troop a few pointers on woodcraft. Archie agreed, and they came to our camp for a pow-wow.

Archie began by showing the boys how and where to find dry wood in wet weather and how to make a quick outdoor fire without an axe. He made them load their arms with twigs, lichen, dead limbs, etc. and said, as he arranged this fodder for the fire, 'When you travel in the bush, remember you must always pay attention to details. You take care of the little things, and the big things will look out for themselves. Here's an example.' He took out his match-safe* from his pocket and held

*a watertight, tin cylinder to keep matches dry.

it out impressively for them to see. 'It's only a little thing, isn't it? Well, many a man would be alive today if he'd carried one of these little do-hickies.'

He lit the fire. 'To carry a rifle with a cartridge in the barrel is a very dangerous thing to do,' he went on. 'It takes but a second to pump one in; you'll lose a second, but you might save your life. And another thing, in running a swift rapids in a canoe, in white water, with rocks and pools ahead – just make one little mistake there and you'll be lucky if you get out of it alive. Maybe you won't be as lucky as you think, because, after all, being in the bush without a canoe is like being up in the air without a plane. Take it from me, it's the little things that count,' he concluded, shaking his finger solemnly at their intent faces. At that moment the fire went 'splut, splut', and ashes and sparks shot up into his face in a cloud. Everyone jumped about, looking to see what had happened. There, on the ground, lay Archie's match-safe, split wide open, right beside the fire.

'Hey, Mr. Belaney,' laughed one of the urchins, 'is that one of the "little things" you were talking about? Ha, ha.'

Of all the times for Archie to pull a greenhorn trick!

We returned to Cabano with over a thousand dollars lining our pockets. The news of how we had got it travelled through the town like wildfire, and those kind and friendly people came to congratulate Archie, as happy for us as if we were their own kin.

There was another letter from *Country Life,* asking Archie to write a book. Although he was rather unnerved concerning this, he replied that he would try to do it.

Dave came to see us as soon as he heard we were back, and was as delighted with our good fortune as our Cabano friends.

'What will you do now?' he asked us.

'I have two tickets to Doucet . . . ' Archie began.

'What!' cried Dave. 'You goin' back dere? Why? Dere's nuttin' dere.'

Archie said, 'You see, we were so damned broke and starved at Metis Beach, all I wanted was to get the hell out of this country before we died of starvation. I was belly-aching about my tough luck to a colonel who was in my outfit during the war. He told me that he would arrange for our fare back north.

I was ashamed, but I was more scared than ashamed, so I took the tickets.' He ended with a wry grin.

'When will you be leaving?' asked Dave sadly.

'When will you be ready?' Archie enquired.

'I can't go,' Dave answered. 'I ain't got the price.'

Archie peeled off some bills. 'You've got the price now – so when are we leaving?'

Dave flicked him a quick grin. 'I feel ashamed too, but I'll take the money.'

We laughed .

'I'm gonna coax you again, Archie,' Dave grew serious. 'Why don't you come with me and stake some claims – up dere where I got dem samples I showed you? It's good stuff, I tell you. And dere's lots of it. Dat country is just full of milliner [minerals]. Oh, c'mon Arch, den we will all get somet'ing outa it.' He showed us the samples once more. They looked spectacular – like gleaming hunks of pure gold. Archie was tempted; he told Dave, 'I'll kick it around for a day or two.'

'Don't take too long,' Dave bellowed happily. 'Freeze-up comes early out dere.' It was already September.

Archie decided to go. What giddy excitement there was in camp as we packed. Even Jelly Roll seemed to sense that something was in the offing, and there surely was, for we were going to the North Pole to stake our bonanza!

But when our gear was loaded on the wagon and we were driving towards the station, we looked back at Elephant Mountain and thought of Mac and Mac. They were with us when we first came, and now we were leaving them forever. We looked at each other, Archie and I, each knowing what the other's thoughts were: one of us, at least, should remain in case Mac and Mac found their way home once more. At the station Archie said, 'I'm sorry, Dave, but I can't go. We're staying here.'

Dave's face fell; he couldn't believe his ears.

'Archie, you go with Dave, I'll stay,' I said.

He shook his head. 'No, I'm going to stay.'

We scrambled into the load and began to sort out our things. While we were doing this, I suddenly made up my mind to go with Dave. There was no time to argue, for the train was pulling in. Archie threw his belongings into the wagon, while I stuffed everything of mine into my pack-sacks. A big audience gathered to watch the performance, for we'd held up the train for twenty minutes with our antics, and all the passengers were gathering around wondering what in hell was going on.

In the rush of our hurried farewells, I had no time to feel anything one way or another.

ΛVΛVΛVΛ

When we arrived in the old, historic city of Quebec, we were told that the train to the north-west of the province wouldn't be leaving until the next day. We didn't want to stay overnight, but there was no alternative. I was in no mood for sightseeing. The reaction to my swift flight had set in, and I was already lonely for Archie and Jelly. The trip had barely begun and here I was fighting the urge to give it up and run home to Archie. Before I did anything rash, I went to my room and wrote him a letter. Dave went to the bar. He spoke French fluently and could get along with the French Canadians very well – too well, in fact. I heard him and several others singing, laughing, and kicking up their heels in the parking-lot at the rear of the hotel about midnight.

In the morning, he was nowhere to be found. I looked into his room and saw that the bed had not been slept in, and here it was, only an hour before train time. Then I recalled that Dave always got religion when in his cups, solemnly singing hymns and saying the mass. Inspired, I ran to the nearest church, thinking he might have found his way there and fallen asleep. No such luck. Nor was he in any of the other places I looked. At last I turned to the police for help.

They suggested that he might be in jail. I hadn't thought of that, and it made me feel worse than if they had said poor Dave had been hung at midnight. They were kind and sympathetic and phoned all the jails in the city, trying to locate him. At each call, they enquired for a tall, slim Indian, about sixty-seven years old. It so happened that there were three tall Indians in the hoosegow that particular day, so I had to accompany the police to look them all over, as the *gendarmes* considered it possible Dave might have given a phoney name. Happily, but unfortunately, none of them turned out to be my quarry. We went to the railroad station on the chance that someone might have seen a man of Dave's description boarding a train. No one had, and the police urged me to return to my husband.

I was stunned by Dave's disappearance. The prospects of a gold mine blasted into thin air. It would take a fortune to re-ship our canoe and camping equipment back to Cabano – both had already gone ahead of us to Oskelaneo. To leave without knowing what had become of Dave was unthinkable. He had very little money with him, and I had both of our tickets. I parked myself at the station, asking everyone in uniform if he had seen Dave, all the while peering desperately down the tracks.

On the second day of his disappearance I finally struck it lucky. A conductor remembered seeing an Indian on his train. He said the man didn't have a ticket, but had told him that 'his little girl' had it and everything would be O.K. But everything was not O.K. Dave had taken the wrong train, going in the wrong direction.

On the third day of my vigil I saw a man hobbling down the track. I was certain that it was old Dave and ran to meet him. Sure enough, it was he. We gave each other a strangling bear-hug, tears streaming down our cheeks. The conductor had taken Dave at his word about 'his little girl' with the ticket and had permitted him to remain on the train. Dave had travelled ninety miles before he became aware of his mistake. He asked the conductor to stop the train so he could start walking back. He refused the chance to return on a freight train, although a kindly section foreman offered to flag one down. When I asked why he didn't accept this offer, he said indignantly, 'A man of my age is not gonna start bummin' rides.' Since he was also too proud to accept food, he hadn't eaten for three days. When he couldn't even take a drink of whiskey, I knew Dave was in a bad way. However, by evening he was able to start eating, so by the time we had travelled to Oskelaneo and at last dipped our paddles into the St. Maurice River, Dave was back to normal and raring to go.

In three weeks time we were at Lac Dore, sixty air miles from Opemiska Lake, where we were to stake our claims. The lake was situated two or three hundred miles south and west of inland Labrador, in rugged, rocky country, very striking in its beauty. Lac Dore was a beehive of activity when we arrived. Clusters of tents loomed all along its shore. Log buildings were going up. There were three diamond-drilling outfits in operation, and we even saw a plane anchored off an island. All of this was a great surprise to Dave. 'I can't understand it,' he said. 'It's not even two years since I passed here, and there was nothing goin' on. Now, just look at it.'

We pulled ashore and set up our tents beside that of a group of prospectors and mining men. Dave wouldn't wait for supper, as he was in a hurry to find out the reason for all the activity. He was back almost immediately, very agitated. 'Pony,' he said, 'some prospectors have made a strike at Opemiska. I'm worried. Maybe they found my stuff.'

'Oh, surely not!' I gasped, feeling a sinking sensation clear down to my boots.

'If I have lost that,' he continued, kicking a log into the fire, 'I'll never be able to face Archie again.' He was the picture of misery.

In an attempt to comfort him, I said, 'Don't worry about that angle. Archie knows that prospecting, in any shape or form, is a gamble. In fact, he told me before we left that I was not to feel badly if nothing came of this trip.'

Dave remained inconsolable. He must have told the men at the other camp the reason we were here, for a Mr. Gillman, a mining man, came rushing into camp and, without any preliminaries, spread a map on the ground and asked Dave where he'd found the mineralized rock that he had mentioned.

Dave was so wrought up I thought he was talking too much, but I didn't know how to say 'shut up' in Algonquin. The outcome was that, as Dave explained to me, 'This man is gonna take us on a plane to where we are headed. By the looks of things I'd say the sooner the better. He says the country is crawling with prospectors.'

I didn't care for the idea of taking a stranger so completely into our confidence. After all, there wasn't a thing, other than a bullet in the head, to prevent him from doing us out of everything.

The next morning we took off – my first flight. I thought this method of transportation really beat the pants off paddling. The plane had an undercarriage for a canoe so, when we landed, we shifted ourselves into the canoe and paddled up a creek for four or five miles and there made a landing. It was the sloppiest pulling-ashore I had ever experienced. In a frenzy Dave plopped the load on shore and pulled the canoe out of the water and just left it right-side up. Nervous as a cat, he led us through the bush and over rocks, practically at a gallop. Finally he turned and said, 'We're just about dere.' Suddenly he stopped. There before him stood a stake post! What we had come so far to stake was already staked. The post was dated twenty-eight days before. Two brothers – aero-prospectors, a new type of prospector at that time – had spotted the outcropping from the air. The claims they staked sold later for $70,000. So we missed a fortune by twenty-eight days.

I shall always remember Dave's disappointment. There was nothing to laugh about, for we were 180 miles, at least, from the railroad. All our time and money had gone for nothing. Ice was now forming on the smaller lakes. It was too late in the season to get out of the country before freeze-up. We could only wait until it froze up properly and then walk out on snow-shoes, but our provisions wouldn't last that long, especially when butter at the Hudson's Bay post was $1.75 a pound. We didn't stand a ghost of a chance.

I was worried. 'Take it easy,' said Dave. When faced with a tough situation, he wasted no time in fretting. The moment we returned to Lac Dore he got a job as a hunter, supplying three diamond-drilling camps with fish, moose and caribou meat. To Dave the problem of eating was solved, but to me the idea of living off the old fellow's hard-earned cash was unthinkable.

Although Lac Dore had a sheet of thin ice along the shore in the early mornings, seaplanes continued to come and go, taking load after load of mining men and prospectors out before winter set in, leaving behind only the drilling crews – and us.

If we could have started the journey earlier, we would have taken a lighter load, thus enabling us to make the trip in, stake the claims, and be out again before freeze-up. But Dave had known that we'd be caught by the coming winter, so we had brought along snowshoes, toboggan, winter clothing, a sack of traps, etc. This extra weight and Dave's 'detour' in the city had slowed us down by at least ten days – ten days that we could well have used now, for we could have made it back to civilization in that time, if we had travelled day and night. This was a lost cause now. Winter was staring us in the face.

'Don't look so sour,' said Dave. 'Dere's nothin' to worry about. Nothin' at all. Before nightfall I'll find a shack. Dere's lots of dem empty now. Dere all leavin'.'

'What do you want a shack for?' I asked, irritably. 'Surely you don't expect to hunt around here with all this noise.'

'Oh, the shack's for you,' he replied.

'I'm supposed to walk right into somebody's shack and just stay there?' I asked.

'Well, yes,' he said.

'Do you mean that I'm supposed to walk into somebody's shack . . . ' I was repeating myself.

'W-e-l-l,' he shrugged uncomfortably.

'Do you mean that I am supposed to . . . ' I began again, idiotically.

'Yes, you're damn right,' he flared. Then he whirled around, got into the canoe, and paddled furiously for Merril Island, where one of the camps he was to supply with meat was situated.

As far as I was concerned, the first thing to be done was to build a shelter. I knew that I wasn't going to starve, and it would take but a short time to throw up a shack-tent, like Sunset Lodge. Still, I wasn't in a glow of happiness. O.K., I would build a shack-tent, but I was *not* going to sit on my hands and wait for Dave to bring home the bacon and earn the money to pay my fare out by plane. One hundred and eighty dollars! No, the only road open to me was to walk out to Oskelaneo, eighty miles, and work my way back to Cabano.

I knew that Archie hadn't any money to send me.

The trouble was that there were several rivers to cross between Lac Dore and Oskelaneo. Some were very swift and would take longer than the lakes to freeze over solid enough to walk on. My grub would be gone by then, even with Dave away and tight rations. If I did accept Dave's assistance, wouldn't it be money made directly from the kill? Something had to be done, and right away. My gaze wandered over Dave's sack of traps. This time my eyes lingered longer. If I went trapping, my worries would be over. I could then write my own ticket to Archie's door. But many animals would have to die to put me on easy street.

I remembered the poor, tortured lynx, the last animal I had trapped, and the one that made me quit the hunt, swearing I would never trap again. I could see no other course, however.

When Dave came back, I asked, 'Are you going to be using your traps?'

'No, I don't think so. I'll be too busy huntin'. Say, do you know dey pay twenty-eight cents freight on every pound dat come in? When ya figure out dat a moose weighs over a thousand pounds, ya can see how much I'm gonna save dem. . . .'

'Then can I have your traps?' I broke into his ramblings to ask.

'Yes,' he said, without thinking. Then, knowing my feelings on trapping, he cried, 'What are ya talkin' about?'

I got the map and pointed to an area. 'This is a creek or a small river. That's where I'm going to get some mink.'

'Don't talk so crazy,' Dave said. 'You just keep warm and hang tough. I'll get ya on the first plane after freeze-up. The least I can do for Archie is to send ya back to him.'

'No, Dave. My mind is made up, if only I knew what to do about a canoe. You'll need one and so will I.'

After a long session of coaxing and arguing about my trapping, Dave gave up and said that he could get a canoe from Chibougamau Prospectors Ltd., one of the drilling outfits he worked for. I was all for pulling out in the middle of the night, so I could begin putting up the log walls for my shack-tent, but Dave refused to listen. So I curled up in my sleeping-bag and thought of Archie and Jelly Roll. I wondered what Archie was doing. Had he found the little dream lake that we had in mind for Jelly Roll and all the other beaver? If he had, would it be as safe and free from danger as we'd hoped? Or maybe he couldn't find the place – our ideal spot, as we called it. If not, he'd have to hurry, with winter almost upon him. Oh, sure, he must have found the right spot by now. He'd just be putting the finishing touches upon his new cabin! I could almost smell the tangy resin. It reminded me of our cabin at Birch Lake, where McGinty and McGinnis had lived with us. Where, oh where did they go? If only I knew! And where are Archie and Jelly?

I know! They're behind Elephant Mountain . . . Archie has found the sanctuary . . . our beaver will be safe . . . Oh God! and tomorrow I will go trapping!

Early the next morning Dave went to the island to get a canoe, and I took my packs, traps, rifle, etc. down to the shore to be ready to go. I was sharpening my axe when Dave came back.

'We got some luck,' he said, grinning from ear to ear. 'Dey tell me dat dere is an old trapper's shack down where you're goin' – so, now ya won't have to build one.'

'Good!' I exclaimed, grinning right back.

Then, handing me a box, he said, 'The cook sent dis to ya. Dey sure feel sorry for ya over dere.'

'Why?'

'Dey t'ink it's awful for a girl to go in trappin' all alone. Dey say it's pitiful – and dangerous.'

I made no comment, as I was thinking about the shack.

'C'mon, open the box,' said Dave.

I lifted the lid, and there in a nest of cookies was a cake, and to the side was a raisin pie and a heap of doughnuts. What a beautiful sight! For a moment, it brought back memories of happier times.

Dave helped me load the canoe, and we said good-bye.

It was pretty dusky by the time I reached the end of the lake and went in search of the cabin that was supposed to be there. I couldn't locate it. It was only when I went deeper into the woods for tent-poles that I saw its dim outline in the shadows of the spruce. It was an old shack, as Dave had said. All the chinking had long gone, the door, minus a hinge, hung at an angle, and the floor-poles were warped and out of place; but the glass in the one window was, incredibly, intact.

Standing there in the gloomy darkness, looking through the gaping walls was like looking through the rib-cage of a skeleton, and the thought that the man who had built the cabin was likely buried somewhere around there gave me a spooky feeling. I left the shack, heartily wishing that it weren't there.

I awakened to a brisk autumn morning, and there is nothing so invigorating; it made short shrift of the cobwebs and ghosts of the night before. I went sprinting over to see what shape the roof of the shack was in, and found that it was in much better condition than I'd thought. I decided to fix it up and began by knocking the bark off the walls and ceiling. Using a stiff broom of spruce boughs, I whisked the dust and clinging bits of bark from every nook and cranny. Then I washed the whole issue down with soap, ashes, and water. When they dried, the logs turned to a delicate shade of mauve, and with the repairs done and its fresh chinking of moss, it was just a dandy shanty.

At dawn one morning, with my camping equipment in the canoe, I started out on the mink hunt. There was now about a foot of snow, and the lake was rimmed by some fifty feet of ice; however, the river was open. To make a long story short, I set trap after trap until it got too dark to see any more. Sick at heart and thoroughly disgusted with myself for doing what I was doing, I went to bed without supper.

There I lay, trying to keep from thinking that at that very moment some animal might be crying out in pain and trying desperately to get away from that cruel thing, the trap – my trap! I got up from my bed of boughs, broke camp, loaded the canoe, and waited for the first light of day, when I was away to pick up every single trap I had set. Fortunately, there wasn't anything in any of them. Fortunately? To me it meant a hike out of Oskelaneo on – if I was lucky – a starvation diet.

I returned to the shack, and on the morning of the first solid ice, I started on the trip out to Oskelaneo. I must admit I hated leaving the security of the old shack.

The first stop was to be Merril Island, where I hoped to see Dave and get some idea of the winter route out. Should he not be there, I would then have to go to the Hudson's Bay factor at Lake Chibougamau, eight miles to the south, to get the necessary information. It was seventeen miles to Merril Island, but on glare ice – one step ahead, two steps back – it added up to fifty-one miles.

When I got there, I walked up to a door sporting the sign OFFICE. Mr. Bell (this isn't his real name), the engineer in charge, answered my knock. I had no sooner introduced myself when he lit into me, hammer and tongs. 'You have no right,' he said, frowning fiercely, 'to go worrying people. A little girl, in the bush, trapping alone, for chrissake.' I hadn't known that they were worried.

The supper gong sounded. Saved by the bell.

127

I asked about Dave, and Mr. Bell said that he'd just left. I turned, opened the door, and stepped out.

'Where are you off to now?' asked Mr. Bell warily.

'I'm going to set up the tent.'

'I'll not have you sleeping out in this kind of weather,' said Mr. Bell, and striding across the floor to a room he continued, 'Reg won't be here till God knows when. You are welcome to this room.'

I thanked him and was about to go and get my bed-roll, when Mr. Bell said that it could wait till after supper.

The crew was still in the dining-room when we entered, and, since I was a stranger, all eyes focussed on me. I hadn't figured on this, and I felt like the proverbial worm in a dish of salt. Even though I thought Mr. Bell a grouch, I was glad he was with me.

The only conversation during the meal was when Mr. Bell asked when I would be going back to my shack. The poor fellow all but choked on his chop when I said that I was on my way to Oskelaneo.

'Of course, you're joking,' he said.

I let it go at that. Mr. Bell was from Arizona, and the evening passed all too quickly as I sat listening to his experiences in South America, Egypt, and other places.

The next morning, after breakfast, I was lashing up the toboggan tarp when Mr. Bell came and asked, 'What's all the rush?'

'I've got around 200 miles ahead of me, so I'd better get going.'

'Did you really mean that about Oskelaneo?'

'Yes.'

'Why, that's suicidal!' he said and dragged me up the steps into the office. Once inside, he told me to wait there until he returned. He came back with a man, and by way of introducing us he said, 'This is Bill. He's the foreman, and wants to ask you something.'

'Yes?'

'We're terribly short-handed here, and we won't be able to get any help until the planes start coming in after freeze-up. So would you like a job?'

'Yes, I'd like a job. What kind of job?'

128

'We need a core-grabber – think you can handle it?'

'Oh sure!' I said, not having the faintest idea of what a core-grabber was. (Slang for core-checker, one who takes the core from the drill rod as it comes up from underground and places it into boxes holding twenty-five feet of core.)

'O.K., you're hired.' He asked my name and, on a sheet of paper, along with many other names, he wrote, 'G. Belaney, Labourer. $5.00 per day.'

In his concern over my welfare, Mr. Bell forgot that they had no accommodation for me. I certainly couldn't stay in the office with him day after day, much less night after night. They built me a shack-tent, which the chore-boy was to fire up all night, as he did all the other quarters. Boy oh boy, what luxurious living!

What incredible luck. Now I would be able to earn my fare back to Archie and Jelly Roll – I would fly back!

The next morning I entered the cook-house for breakfast as one of the crew. There were thirty-four of us, and the rest of the crew was as embarrassed as I. After breakfast, the foreman came to me and said, 'Come over to my shack, and I'll show you the ropes.'

When we got there, I saw two men hammering at something held down in a vise. I learned later that they were adjusting or replacing industrial diamonds in the drill bits. Bill, the foreman, immediately got down to business by asking, 'Can you handle dogs?'

'Oh sure,' I answered with emphasis, for I knew what a dog was, but what was a core-grabber?

'Well,' said Bill, 'if it's all right with you, I'd just as soon you work with the dogs.'

'It's O.K. with me – what do you want me to do with the dogs?'

'There's a wood-cutter across the bay. Now if you will just go and harness up those five big dogs out there and haul in a bunch of wood, that'll be just fine.'

I hauled wood all morning, a quarter-cord a load, then did the same thing in the afternoon, except for the times when I was asked to take twenty gallons of gas to that drill and twenty to another drill. Before the day was over, I knew that this job wasn't going to be a whiz, but I was glad because I knew I was earning my money. (I had a suspicion that Mr. Bell had hired me only to save my life; he thought I would have died on the way out to Oskelaneo.)

Our jobs, the dogs and mine, consisted of supplying thirteen stoves, which burned twenty-four hours a day, with wood; and three drills, each operating twenty-four hours a day, with gas; and when the planes came in, the dogs and I had to take care of the freight – tons of it.

'Why don't you take five once in a while?' Mr. Bell said to me one day.

I told him that I tried that and ended up by being late for supper. 'Oh come now, kid. you haven't that much to do.'

There were several letters from Archie on the first plane that came in after freeze-up. I took Dave's advice not to tell Archie what I was doing, because if he knew I was working with a bunch of men and living in the same camp, it would drive him crazy, and it was just as well that I didn't tell him, for Archie's letters were full of worry as it was. What I managed to glean from Archie's letters was that there was still no sign of Mac and Mac, and that he had not built a cabin, but was living in an abandoned lumber camp. He had, however, found a little lake, just the right size for Jelly. He was keeping at the book (this was when he was writing *The Men of the Last Frontier*.) He had written an article for a Canadian outdoor magazine, which had been accepted, but he hadn't as yet received any money from it, and he would send my fare home as soon as he could.

I'd been so elated at getting the job that the thought of being afraid of the men didn't occur to me. They didn't at any time give me cause to fret. By now I knew them all by their first names, and I had even got into some of their games. They thought it quite a joke when I lost twenty-one dollars learning to play, of all games, blackjack. That came out of my first cheque. I stuck to my knitting after that.

One mild evening, I stopped in at one of the bunk-houses wearing a simple lady's blouse (one I'd brought from home). Well, the hullabaloo that caused! They whooped and hollered 'Look, look – Pony's wearing a bathing suit. Oh, ain't she great!' Then someone suggested that I ought to have make-up as well. 'I've got the powder,' yelled Marcel, coming towards me. Round and round the stove we went, till McCormack caught me and held me while Marcel all but drowned me with his talcum powder.

Three p.m. Christmas Eve the camp was in a near riot, because half the crew intended going out for the holidays, but the plane had failed to come in. I was especially sorry for Mr. Bell, because his wife and family were coming all the way from Arizona to spend the Yuletide season with him at Roberval.

It was growing dark, and the men, cussing and swearing, paced about like caged tigers. Then, at four p.m., we heard the drone of a plane, and we all but fell over ourselves scrambling down to the lake to meet it. The plane was unloaded in jig time, for those who were impatient to take off dumped the stuff off like dirt, that is, except for one large item – a sixty-gallon barrel of beer.

'For heaven's sake, who sent that in?' asked Mr. Bell, astonished.

'The Chibougamau Prospectors,' said the pilot.

'Like hell they did!' exclaimed Mr. Bell.

A barrel of beer? And freight at twenty-seven cents a pound. Of course, somebody had made a lovely mistake. There wasn't time to argue, so Mr. Bell turned to me and said, 'Get some help and roll that up to the office. Dish it out as you see fit.'

They took off. Wishing terribly that I was on the plane, I watched it till it was out of sight, leaving, except for a few blinking stars, an empty sky. Mr. Bell had given me orders to stay in the office to look after the canteen while he was away, so when the freight had been cleared from the lake, I sat down in the office and began sorting the mail.

I'd no sooner started sorting letters than the men came filing in for their mail, so I pushed the stack over and told them to help themselves – there were several letters from Archie, and I was anxious to read them. I also told them to take a couple of pails of beer over to their bunk-houses.

There being no lack of food or spirits, we had a merry Christmas and a happy start on 1930. However, two weeks after the holidays there was still no plane from the outside, and it was splendid flying weather. We began to wonder. We had no engineer and no foreman, and lacking a full crew we had only one drill in operation. Had they crashed? No, but the world stock market had.

This was the first news Mr. Bell told me when he arrived on the much-awaited plane. Of course I didn't understand the significance of this, but I could see that Mr. Bell was greatly agitated, and he said, 'I'm going right back on that plane – I've just come for my gear. The way things are out there, you'll be lucky if you get your wages – they're a month behind already. If I were you, I'd haul out a bunch of flour, sugar, lard, tea, anything that you can lay your hands on, and cache it somewhere. . . .'

'Why?' I interrupted.

'So you can trade it in furs with the Indians when they come in in the spring. That's the only way you'll get your wages from this outfit.' I couldn't imagine myself sneaking to the storehouse in the dead of night and stealing load upon load of flour, etc. Mr. Bell's last words were 'You'd better go after that stuff before they come in and take an inventory.'

Then Gillman, the promoter of Chibougamau Prospectors Ltd., came in late in January and shut the whole shebang down. The plane waited for the men to pack, and suddenly they were all gone. I still hadn't been paid. I'd had only two weeks' wages out of this company so far, but Mr. Gillman said not to worry, that he would pay me out of his own pocket. Unfortunately, he didn't have the money with him. If he'd had it, I would have been on that plane flying home to Archie and Jelly Roll.

Gillman appointed me caretaker, and he said before he left, 'Sell everything and anything that you can.' But there were no buyers! Well, at least I wouldn't have to steal, as Mr. Bell had suggested. They didn't bring any mail this trip, so no word from Archie.

Luckily, there were three prospectors living on the north shore. Though there was plenty to read and I had a radio and the dogs for company, I must admit it was lonely on the island. My loafing didn't last too long, thank goodness, for out of the blue came a plane, bringing a man who said his company had bought all the gas and drill rods from the Chibougamau Prospectors Limited. He asked me if I would haul the stuff to the drill at Antoinette Lake. They couldn't fly the material over to the site because the lake was very small, and it was difficult for planes to land there and still harder for them to take off. I took the job.

The three prospectors who lived on the north shore had been going back and forth to their claims on Antoinette Lake, so I would have a fine trail to start with. They warned me, however, that there was a bad hog's-back on the way. Well, what's a hog's-back? I took 600 pounds on the first trip. This was a mistake.

We, the dogs and I, sailed merrily along at a frisky clip all morning; then suddenly we rammed smack into the hog's-back. It was higher than a barn and twice as steep. With me pushing and the dogs pulling for all we were worth, we managed to inch the load up. To my disgust and dismay, I found the ridge to be as steep on the other side, so I unhitched the dogs and reversed the sleigh and, using a pole as a brake, I took the load down backwards. Straining against 600 pounds at a fifty-degree angle takes some doing – and at twelve cents a pound I was earning my money. The dogs were barking and yelping and jumping over and around the load, poking their noses under my hood and licking my face. It was plain to see that they wanted to help.

At last the freighting was over with and I had more than enough money to go to Cabano, but there were no planes coming in. Finally, on the first of June, Gillman came, and I told him I wasn't going to stay a minute longer. 'Pay me now,' I said. 'I'm going home on that plane.' He did, and I was on the plane within the hour.

I had a six-hour wait in the city of Quebec (the rest of the journey was to be by train) so I went on a shopping tour. I got Archie a pipe and a supply of his favorite Edgeworth tobacco, several bottles of Johnny Dewar's Extra Special, and a stack of clothes for us both. Then I went to my first talkie, *The Floradora Girl*. Wasn't that something! After almost a year in the north, this little bushwhacker was plenty thrilled and dazzled by all this.

I arrived in Cabano and went straight to our friends the Grahames. After receiving a hearty welcome and answering a thousand and one questions, I was able to enquire about Archie. No, they hadn't seen him in nearly a month. This struck a

133

sinister note, and I became uneasy. I wanted to go to him immediately, but I didn't know where he was. I had to locate a Frank Burbe to take me in, for he knew where Archie was situated, and the Grahames kindly offered to find Burbe for me.

In the meantime I went to the store to buy things to eat, for I wanted our reunion to be as festive as it could be. The Grahames located Frank Burbe, and he and I were soon on our way to Archie.

Archie was sitting at the table when I came to the opened door. I had no intention of making this a surprise party – I only walked quietly to the cabin because I was afraid of what I might find. 'Archie,' I called, scarcely above a whisper, but the way he sprang up one would have thought that a bomb had exploded.

'Gurdy!' was all he said. We stood as if rooted and just looked at each other. Then I dropped my pack to the ground and ran to him, and we held each other close for the longest time. We hadn't yet said a word except each other's names. Then there was a polite cough from the door. It was Frank. I'd completely forgotten about him.

'C'mon Archie,' I said, going to the pack-sacks. 'Let's loot the loot.'

It was a joy to see Archie's delight and appreciation as he opened his gifts. Holding a pair of trousers up, trying them for length, he said 'I suppose I ought to say, "Oh, you shouldn't have" – blah, blah – but I can't because I'm glad that you did.' I loved Archie's wholehearted acceptance of gifts.

Then Jelly Roll crashed the party, and when she remembered me my happiness was complete.

Archie then told me there was a new addition to the family. A beaver had been caught in a trap he had set in June to protect Jelly Roll from a marauding otter. (An otter is sudden death to young beaver.) Archie took the animal out of the trap and brought him home to attend to his wounded foot. The beaver had gashed his head in his struggle to escape the trap, and when the cut had healed, there was a piece of dried skin hanging from the scalp, which Archie had clipped – and for this reason Archie called him Rawhide. Rawhide became so tame he slept contentedly by Archie's side and would put up a great hue and cry whenever Archie went out the door.

I'd been home five months. It was already November, and I was happy to be there, but living with a person who is writing is worse than being alone. One feels that one must tiptoe at all times and check any spontaneous outburst of conversation, so when Archie told me that the book couldn't possibly be ready before January at the earliest, I had to admit to myself that I couldn't face another week, let alone two more months, of this morgue-like atmosphere. When I told him I was leaving, he said:

'I know how dead it is for you 'round here. I realize this more than you think. In fact, if it wasn't for this thing [the book], which I am beginning to hate, I'd go completely nuts. I was thinking that if I could make a dicker with Mrs. Grahame, you could go and stay there, where there are people and things. Would you like that?'

'I don't think so. Anyhow, where will we get the money for board and room?'

'That's what I mean. If Mrs. Grahame will take a chance on my selling the book, she'll get paid; if not . . . . ' He let it go at that.

Somehow, I just couldn't see this as the solution, so I decided to go to Montreal and see Gillman, who, I was sure, would send me up north on another job. Before I left, Archie promised that he would send for me if he needed help with the beaver, or if ever he became sick.

When I arrived in Montreal, Gillman didn't have a thing to offer me as far as work was concerned, but he did have a suggestion.

He said, 'There is a brand-new summer and winter resort they've just opened in Montebello – it's forty miles east of Ottawa; you might get work there.'

'Doing what?' I wondered.

'Say, what about a team of dogs? Surely they've got them for the guests – they've apparently got everything else,' said Gillman.

'Then that's what I'll do!' I said, as if it were all settled, but Gillman said, 'Hey, wait a minute, keep your feet on the ground. There's a depression on, remember.'

However, he put in a long-distance call to Montebello. No, they didn't have dogs. Oblivious to everything, I sat and stared at Gillman in my despair.

'Well, don't just sit there,' he said as he handed me an address. 'Go and see this fellow. He's a big wheel in that outfit; sell him on the dog idea. I'd take you there myself, but, as you see, I'm a working man now.' As he ended, he spread his hands in disgust. He hated being cooped up in an office.

The lodge was a very plush affair. The decor ran to mounted heads of buffalo, moose, elk, and caribou, and on the walls were the pelts of wolverine, badger, lynx, foxes, and wolves. The chairs and lounges were draped with Navajo blankets, and the floors were covered with buffalo and polar-bear rugs. The main attraction of the lodge was its six fireplaces; there was a hexagonal chimney with a fireplace at the base of each face in the centre of the rotunda, so that nobody was left out in the cold.

The winter sports consisted of skiing, riding, tobogganing, and bob-sledding. Because of the scenic route of our trail, the dogs came to be in great demand with the guests. There was a full house on New Year's Eve, and champagne flowed like 'moose milk'. It was all very gay. People from as far away as New York and Vancouver came to see Nels Nelson, then the world's champion skier, take the 263-foot ski-jump on New Year's Day.

On Christmas Eve, our boss had said that we of the sports staff were to bring in the New Year and take out the old, so as midnight approached, we were outside of the lodge, taking our places for the march around the fireplace. Nels, on skis, was to lead the parade; after him would come the ski instructors, also on skis, followed by the toboggan and bob-sled pilots with a toboggan and sled; then the riding major and finally the dogs with the 'New Year', a cute, curly-headed infant, in the carriole.

The idea was that when we entered the lodge, a bewhiskered chap (the Old Year) would appear to take the infant from the carriole to Nels, who was to carry him on the march. The 'Old Year' was then to take the baby's place in the carriole. To complete the performance, the dogs were to circle the room once, then out the door we would go with the 'Old Year'. It was down pat.

At the stroke of midnight the doors were flung open. I cracked the whip and hollered 'Mush'.

WELCOME 1931! But the dogs had no sooner entered the foyer and 'Old Year' taken 'New Year' in his arms, than someone turned off the lights. The only illumination was the dim lights from the fireplaces. Then, amidst the blare of horns and whistles and all the other unimaginable noisemakers, and the guests shouting 'Happy New Year' and singing, the dogs went wild. They circled the room to beat old hell, the carriole barely skimming the floor, then out the door we went – leaving the 'Old Year' behind.

Time flew after the New Year. Then one night in February I received a telegram from Archie asking me to meet him in Montreal, at once. I was to go to the Windsor Hotel and ask for Grey Owl.

I arrived in Montreal the next morning and was taken to Archie's suite, where I found him with Sir Charles Delmé Radcliff. (Sir Charles had volunteered to see to our needs while we were in Montreal.) At the first chance I asked, 'Archie, what are we doing here?'

'I accepted an invitation to be guest speaker at the Canadian Forestry Association's annual convention. I figured that before I was through I'd be in dire need of moral support – that's why I sent for you.'

To lecture in Metis Beach was one thing, but in Montreal it was an entirely different thing, and I began to shake in my boots. Our nerves suffered the entire gamut of stage fright as we waited for zero hour. Even Sir Charles was jumpy when the time came.

However, we needn't have gone through all that hell, because the lecture was a great, great success. The audience would not let Archie go. When, at last, it was over, people came to us and said such nice things. An elderly gentleman said, as he shook Archie's hand, 'I don't know whether I have just heard a poem or an encyclopedia on wildlife.'

When the last of the well-wishers had gone, Sir Charles was

waiting for us with a couple whom he introduced as a Mr. and Mrs. Flagstone. Archie, in a hurry to get back to the security of the room, merely acknowledged the introduction, and we left.

The following morning Sir Charles came, carrying a news-paper. It was obvious that he was greatly agitated. Then, show-ing us the front page with a picture of Archie and me that had been taken after the lecture, Sir Charles whacked the paper with the back of his hand and said, 'Just look at Anahareo – isn't it ghastly!' Since I had a cold at the time, my face looked like a boxing-glove. Then he pointed to the heading across the page. It read, in box-car letters: FULL-BLOODED INDIAN GIVES LECTURE ON WILDLIFE.

'And what are you going to do about that?' asked Sir Charles, pointing at the heading.

Archie said, 'Why nothing, why spoil their little old story?'

Had Archie known how seriously people were going to take his ancestry, this would have been the time to have clamped down on that 'full-blooded Indian' stuff. But how was he to know that the more he wrote, the more Indian he became in the eyes of the public?

Dropping the subject, Sir Charles said, 'By the way, you and Anahareo are invited to the Flagstones for dinner tonight.'

'The Flagstones?' Archie, wrinkling his brow, tried to place them. Then he said, 'Oh, them . . . you'll never catch me going there.'

'What is this?' asked Sir Charles, not believing his ears.

'No sir, I wouldn't go there, even if it was to be my last chance to eat. I won't go.'

'And why won't you go?' asked Sir Charles.

'I judge the man to be the condescending type, and her, she's packing a superiority complex as big as a barn. In spite of all that gushing, I don't take her to be sincere. No thank you, I'm not going.'

'You are away out, Grey Owl,' said Sir Charles. 'Why, they are among the finest people I know.'

Maybe I am just a frustrated social-climber, but I suddenly had an overwhelming desire to dine at the Flagstones' and to that end went to work on Archie, hammer and tongs, with Sir Charles. Between us we broke down Archie's resistance, and he consented to go, but not without having the last word.

'I know the type well,' he said. 'All they want is a little fun at our expense. They'll expect me to drink from the finger-bowl and wash up in the soup. They'll get more than they bargained for.'

'Oh, I say, if that is the way you feel about it, I'll see what I can do,' said Sir Charles, much concerned.

Archie, adopting the role of a martyr, said, 'No, I'll go. I said I'd go, and I'll go.'

And we did.

Of course, the Flagstones lived in a magnificent mansion. The lights coming from the many windows reminded me of the Chateau Frontenac. The very sight of the imposing structure scared the wits out of me, and I began to wish I hadn't come.

At the door Archie turned and said, 'I'm warning you – you aren't going to like this.'

'Why?'

'Because.'

I will never forget the startled expression on the butler's face when he opened the door. 'Oh,' he gasped and jumped back at least four feet. I guessed that he had never been at such close quarters with an Indian and I felt sorry for him. My sympathies, however, were short-lived, for the butler, having regained his composure, was surveying us with undisguised amusement and contempt. There wasn't time for Archie to wipe that smirk off his face, because the Flagstones were coming forward to greet us; that is, they were till they stopped short in their tracks. They too, I thought, expected us to turn up in 'soup and fish.'

'If that's the way they want it, that's the way they're going to have it!' Archie whispered viciously. Archie, believing these people thought him an ignoramus, evidently was going to act the part.

Archie, turning to the butler who had been waiting for his hat, handed it to him, but snapped it back again. He repeated this performance several times. The man was getting into a nasty temper. Again Archie handed over the hat. This time the butler shot his hand out, like a snake, and got a firm grip. He thought he had it, but Archie gave it a neat jerk and got it back again. Then Archie let it drop to the floor and stood expectantly, waiting for the butler to pick it up. Just as the butler stooped, so did Archie, and 'bang' went their heads. The resounding crash echoed ridiculously around the cavernous hall. The Flagstones came running to our rescue. They said something to the butler, who immediately went skulking away. Archie let him go with never a word in his defense.

In the drawing-room the scene was the exact opposite, for it wasn't what Archie did, it was what he didn't do. For instance, he sat there, looking like Sitting Bull. He spoke but once, and that was 'Thanks' when he was handed a highball. We moved to the dining-room, and at the table Archie kept looking over his shoulder at the major domo, who was standing well back.

'Isn't he going to eat?' Archie murmured in a low voice, indicating the waiter with his thumb.

'The servants dine before we do,' Mrs. Flagstone graciously informed him.

'Yeah, I suppose after working all day they'd get hungrier quicker.' So saying, he grappled with his table napkin and was about to tuck it in his collar, when he stole a glance at the host, not too obviously, but with sufficient fuss to make sure they would notice. Then, looking guilty, he dropped it to his lap. (This, of course, was part of the act.) Mr. Flagstone opened the conversation.

'Well, Grey Owl, what do you think of our town?' he began bravely.

Archie, wagging his head slowly and sadly, said, 'I just can't figure out how anybody can live in a place like this.'

'Why, what do you mean?' asked Mr. Flagstone.

'For one thing, there's too much noise, and too many people, and there's no short cuts.' This inane reply was greeted with polite laughter.

Mrs. Flagstone said, 'Yes, I can well understand your point of view,' and turning to me said, 'From your husband's lecture last evening, which I positively a-dore-d, you must live a most extra-ordinary life in the woods. . . .'

Before I could answer, Archie launched into a discussion of the city, as he saw it, and during the time of speaking his napkin dropped three times to the floor; each time he disappeared out of sight to retrieve it. He finally jammed it into his pocket.

Of all Archie's idiotic behaviour that night, the most nerve-wracking was his by-play with the cut glass. The water glass, as he talked, kept gradually sidling towards the edge of the table.

What with his arms flying as he talked, it had several close calls, and at last it happened. Off went the glass! Archie scooped it up in mid-air. The trick was performed with the grace and rhythm of a master juggler. He plunked the glass back on the table and said, 'How do you like that for co-ordination?'

I could have killed him! But I only kicked him, none too gently.

'Gurdy,' he said imploringly, 'I wish you wouldn't keep kicking me under the table like that.'

'I was doing the same thing to Jack – he keeps interrupting Grey Owl so,' said Mrs. Flagstone, lying beautifully. In the ensuing silence we feigned interest in our food. Things were seemingly too quiet down Archie's way, and I glanced up uneasily. A little groan attracted the attention of the others. What do you suppose? It appeared that Archie's fork was stuck in his mouth; he was twisting the fork this way and that, but without results. Then he pressed his knife, ever so gently, against his delicately raised pinky – then threw his head back and the fork was out. The ridiculous stunt was so neatly executed, and was so obvious, that everyone at the table hooted and laughed.

'Superb,' the host exclaimed. 'I wouldn't have missed that technique for anything. What a devil you are, Grey Owl!'

The ice was broken; Archie apologized for his outrageous behaviour and told them why he had done it.

'I must confess, Grey Owl, that you threw me. After all, for a man who could hold an audience as you did last night, I rather expected something different – if not intellectual, at least congenial,' said Mr. Flagstone, grinning.

'That just goes to show you,' said Archie, 'that those snap judgements of mine aren't worth a hoot in hell.'

'Yeah,' agreed Mr. Flagstone. 'I'm still carrying scars from doing the same thing.'

Remembering the shocked expression on Mrs. Flagstone's face when we came in, I said, 'I am awfully sorry to have scared you – coming to dinner in buckskins like this.' I had never been so clothes-conscious.

'Scared?' she asked. 'Why you poor dear, what nonsense! You simply took my breath away – you and Grey Owl made such a striking picture standing there with your bea-u-tiful fringed jackets and all. Really, I don't think that *anything* could be as becoming on you as what you've got on – or could it?' With a mischievous gleam in her eye, she led me to her boudoir.

'We'll let those gazabos talk their heads off – but let's have a time of our own.' She hesitated and then added, 'Would you like to try on some of my things?' Would I? Well, I guess! Her wardrobe was large, and, needless to say, beautiful. I tried on frock after frock. Some were too 'old'; others, the colour wasn't right.

We finally found one, a deep red with black lace, and though she was an inch shorter than I, the gown was a perfect fit. Having styled my hair and made up my face, Mrs. Flagstone was fastening the last piece of jewelry when Mr. Flagstone called for the umpteenth time. She hurriedly donned my buckskins, breeches, and boots, and we sauntered into the living-room. The men rose as we entered and were about to be seated again when they noticed that something was amiss. Their look of astonishment was something to see. Mr. Flagstone went to Mrs. Flagstone and, giving her a hug, said, 'It suits you to a tee, dear – we must get you an outfit just like it.'

Archie, staring at me in amazement, said, 'I had no idea you looked like . . . that.'

'Why Grey Owl, what's the matter? She looks stunning.'

'Yes, I know, but I had no idea that she looked like that. . . .' he repeated stupidly. Later that night, Archie told me I was beautiful. Clothes still make the woman.

Against Archie's protests we stayed in Montreal for another day, and Sir Charles showed us the many interesting things to see in the big city. We were to finish the day off by going to the theatre to see *Africa Speaks,* but when it was time to go Archie said he wasn't feeling well, and insisted that Sir Charles and I go. When we returned at midnight from the movie, Archie had a temperature. Ever since he'd been gassed with mustard gas during the war, colds had raised havoc with him. He refused Sir Charles' suggestion of getting a doctor. By four a.m. Archie was burning up with fever, but he still refused outside help.

In the morning the doctor said that he had pneumonia.

I wired Montebello for my things, because I certainly wasn't going to leave Archie alone in his illness, but he was more concerned over the possibility of some trapper getting Jelly Roll and

Rawhide. 'Please do as I say,' he begged when I refused to leave him. 'I'll be taken care of, but someone will get them, sure as hell.'

There was no use arguing.

Pneumonia was a serious illness before penicillin, and it was terrible being in the bush and unable to get news of his condition.

Then, suddenly, he was back. Having snowshoed the two miles in from the highway, he was at the point of collapse. He literally staggered into the cabin. It was then that he told me that he had been in hospital and that he'd left against his doctor's orders, as soon as he was allowed out of bed. I was scolding him for doing such a stupid thing when he handed me a letter.

The letter was from a representative of the Minister of the Interior of the federal government in Ottawa, stating that Archie now had a position as 'naturalist'. The Minister's offer was of considerable consequence, since it was not only giving us a place to live, but, what was more important, a sanctuary for the beaver. We felt at last we were not striving alone; we had the whole of the Canadian government behind us. The Minister's letter spelled out distinctly that our endeavours would receive all the assistance available.

Our new home was to be in the Riding Mountain National Park in Manitoba. However we would not be able to move there for at least another six weeks, because Jelly Roll and Rawhide were now living in a house of their own, like real beaver, and would be frozen in till April. We couldn't help wondering whether they had reverted to wild beaver. If they had, we were going to have a difficult time capturing them. We wouldn't have worried about Jelly Roll's coming to us, but Rawhide had been a wild beaver for his first two years. Tame as he had become, Rawhide nevertheless could still have wild instincts, and Archie naturally feared that some of them would rub off on Jelly Roll.

Since Archie's book *The Men of the Last Frontier* (originally called *The Vanishing Frontier*) was now in the hands of the publisher and he had only a couple of articles to write for *Forest and Outdoors*, we were, at last, able to enjoy each other's company, and the days flew by on the wind.

Suddenly it was March, and though Jelly Roll and Rawhide were still ice-locked, we commenced to make daily journeys to their house with the idea of getting them used to our voices again. After a week of calling out their names and talking to them from the top of their lodge, we cut a couple of holes in the ice by the feed-raft and put birch and poplar limbs into them. Once the beaver had taken the saplings, we knew it wasn't going to be too difficult to capture them.

This proved to be true, for it wasn't long before they began coming out to us for apples, rice, etc. Finally the day came when we put them into a ventilated tin box, fastened the lid down securely, and hauled them home on the toboggan. We felt like traitors, but they didn't hold it against us for long.

A few days later we left on our journey west. The tin box was again used to transport the beaver to the railroad station, where there was a 4' x 6' tank with bath, a drying-off platform, and an upper tier for living-quarters – a magnificent affair. Our friends, kidding us, said that while he was at it, Archie should have chartered a private coach, or even a train, to take us to Riding Mountain.

I didn't go all the way to Riding Mountain with Archie, because a mining man at Montebello had told me that the Elk Lake country (northern Ontario) was the place to go prospecting. I went as far as Toronto with Archie, and there we parted. He went on his way to the prairies, and I boarded a train that took me over the very same route that Archie had walked on his first venture into the north country to Bill, old Ag-Nu, and Angele.

Since I didn't make a strike, I won't go into the details of that jaunt, except for this: a prospector whose camp was two or three portages away from mine had to rush home because his infant daughter had taken seriously ill. While there, he got news that there had been a recent discovery of gold (at a place now called Val-d'Or) in northern Quebec. He wanted to get there in the shortest time possible to stake claims, so he sent a wire to me, asking that I take his outfit to the half-way. I did. It was a four-day trip, and on my return from this excursion I found that my camp had been struck by lightning and had burned to the ground. So there I stood, with nothing but the clothes that I wore and a canoe.

There was nothing for it but to send an S.O.S. to Archie. When I arrived at the half-way, where I got my mail, there was a telegram and money waiting for me from Archie. The message read, 'Come immediately. I will meet you in Winnipeg – wire when you will be there.'

Not having a thing to pack, I pushed off and didn't let any moss gather on my paddle getting out to the railroad. It was a three-day trip by canoe and three more days by train to Winnipeg, where Archie had said he would meet me; but he was nowhere to be seen.

I must have been a devastating sight, standing on the station platform in my bush clothes, which were rumpled and none too clean – I'd been prospecting in them for weeks before the fire. (We washed only underwear, socks, and occasionally a shirt – never the pants.) Archie had been watching for me down at the Pullman car. I hadn't thought of a berth, so I was fluttering in panic around the day-coach.

Then, suddenly, I was in the warmth and security of his arms.

Winnipeg wasn't home – not by a long-shot – for there was yet a 200-mile journey by train, another 48 miles in a truck to the resort at Riding Mountain Park, and 28 more miles on a wagon.

At long last the horses came to a halt before a building of great dimensions, built of stained and varnished logs. Archie said 'Welcome home.' Of course, I couldn't believe that this beautiful bungalow with its verandah was 'our place', but it was, and I was overjoyed. Compared to anything we'd ever had, this was a castle.

Jelly Roll had had four kittens in May. Because of a drought the little lake had become stagnant and impossible for the beaver. I was to care for our brood of six, while Archie went to Waskesiu in Prince Albert National Park in quest of an ideal spot for Jelly Roll and family. Archie was anxious to leave for Waskesiu and was away the very next morning.

After he'd gone, I took out the plan that he had drawn up of the cabin that the government would build for us, once a site was decided upon. The design of the 14′ x 16′ log cabin would be an architect's nightmare. The specifications were to include not only living-areas for two people, but living-quarters for our family of beaver; and most essentially, a plunge-hole (a submerged tunnel under the foundations, leading out to the beaver's feed-raft in the lake). Our part of the floor, of adzed logs, was to be surrounded by a low fence; the rest was of earth for the beaver. There was also a gateway for them to come and go as they pleased through our part of the cabin.

At first I was heart-broken at the thought of having to leave the bungalow, but when I saw the beaver emerge from the slimy water – the scum so thick it looked like dirty cellophane – I would have cheerfully taken them instantly away.

Archie returned in ten days. Of all the many lakes he'd explored, he had decided that Lake Ajawaan was best suited for our purpose. Lake Ajawaan was located one hundred miles north of Prince Albert, Saskatchewan – seventy miles by car and thirty by water.

Our moving wasn't just a matter of crating the animals and taking off. It entailed much planning. In this case, the weather was of great importance. Because of the beaver's drive to build, they would have to be kept in captivity until Ajawaan froze over. Otherwise, unmindful of the cold, they'd busy themselves in cutting down trees for their winter's food, building a house, and, of course, improving the dam, and this could be fatal for them. Beaver work during the night, and it was quite possible that while they were out of the lake collecting sticks a severe drop in temperature could occur and cause it to freeze over with ice too thick for them to break through. Then they would be locked out for the winter and would soon freeze to death.

We left Riding Mountain on October 26, 1931. It was a worrisome trip, but happily, our family – Jelly Roll, Rawhide, Wakanee and Wakanoo, Silver Bells, and Buckshot – arrived at Ajawaan on the first of November in good condition; only Archie and I weren't!

We named our new home Beaver Lodge. It was there that Rawhide's worries began. Because it was so late in the season and he had no house or food for his family, poor Rawhide became alarmed to the point of insanity.

Though Beaver Lodge couldn't touch the bungalow for class,

it was comfortable. With four playful kitten beaver under foot – those scallywags were everywhere – and Jelly's demands, which were many, and Rawhide's chewing the house down, it was all very lively.

Near the end of November the lake froze over, and it was now safe to let the beaver out. We lifted the barricade to the plunge-hole, and as soon as we did, Rawhide took to it like blue lightning. Now was his chance, he thought, to see to his family's needs; but he was ice-locked and would be until spring. However, having discovered the built-in feed-raft, he returned, excited as could be, with a limb of poplar, which he laid before Jelly Roll. Then he began a great harangue, his voice hitting the high and the low notes, and those in between; I suppose he was telling Jelly not to worry any more, because they would have plenty of grub for the winter. Now that Archie was on a steady salary, we had no cause for worry over our grub situation either – that is, except for fresh meat. However, small game, deer, moose, and caribou would provide us with that, so when the weather was right Archie went north of Pelican Lake, outside of the park boundary, and got a moose.

After the meat situation was taken care of, and we were as settled as we could ever be, there wasn't anything left to do. Archie soon became moody and restless. One night, when he was particularly depressed, he asked bitterly, 'What are we supposed to do now – just sit in a void for the rest of our lives? I'm afraid, in fact, I'm scared sick I'm not going to be able to take it; this inactivity will kill me. The way I'm feeling right now, I hope it does.'

So he raved till he ran out of words that spelled despair. Then he became full of self-reproach for losing sight of the long-dreamed-of beaver colony. After an exceedingly active life, Archie had suddenly come to a dead-end; even his economic worries were taken away. He at least had had those after he quit trapping. And yet, he certainly hadn't been idle after he'd quit the trap-line, for the summer after was spent in his search for McGinty and McGinnis, and in writing *The Men of the Last Frontier,* as well as magazine articles. And following that he had moved the beaver from Quebec to Manitoba and then from there to Ajawaan. Now, to kill time and burn up superfluous energy, Archie often went out on exploring expeditions, frequently staying overnight, and sometimes two or three days. I, on the other hand, was perfectly satisfied to stay home and just loaf, read, listen to the radio, and play with those little scallywags. I was content, but not for long. In January Archie, full of enthusiasm, announced that he was going to write another book.

Instead of being overjoyed, I abhorred the idea. The picture of Archie writing – always in a haze, no companionship whatsoever – flashed before me. 'Oh, please don't do anything like that – not until I can get out of here.'

'Don't be silly. Why, I thought you'd be glad.'

'But I'm not – I'm not,' I shouted angrily. Since there were no jobs to be had on account of the Depression, I'd have nowhere to go. In good times or bad, how many openings are there for a trapper, dog-musher, or prospector? None. My only hope was to go prospecting, but spring was so far off. I was going to be stuck with a zombie all winter. The thought was unbearable, and I was in a fine lather. Archie could see this.

'This isn't going to be like the other book – it'll be nothing serious. I'll just dabble at it when I have nothing else to do.'

'But you *never* have anything to do, so you'll be dabbling all the time – dabble, dabble. . . .' I ended spluttering. Archie laughed and said, 'O.K., kid, let's forget it. . . . It was just a crazy notion I guess.'

I was immediately contrite and ran to him and told him not to pay any attention to my silly objections. But I had dashed his enthusiasm. In the end I was coaxing him, as I had at the Birch Lake cabin, to go on with his writing. He did. He 'dabbled' *Pilgrims of the Wild* right onto the best-seller list.

All I heard from Archie that winter was the scratch, scratch of his pen, and arguments against taking a bath. Like a kid, he loathed baths. Following are some of the excuses he offered.

'A *bath!* In a one-room shack? That's ridiculous . . . I've got to have privacy.'

'I can't – I've got a hell of a cold coming on.' To prove it, there'd be much nose-blowing, coughing, and snorting. Then, 'You're like my aunt – take a bath, take a bath. . . . It's a wonder that I have any skin left. . . .'

Once he asked, 'Do you know what caused the fall of the Roman Empire?'

'No.'

'Hot baths – that's what.'

It was all said in fun, but he'd have got out of it if he could.

There had been many times, when I was prospecting, that I'd wished I knew more about rocks, so while Archie was writing *Pilgrims,* I took a correspondence course in mineralogy.

So engrossed were we in what we were doing that when meal-times came we visited as though we hadn't seen each other in days.

By now the beaver had built a house of their own. We looked on in pity at its initial stages, for it began with a few sticks that leaned against the wall over the plunge-hole. Of course, we thought that nothing would ever come of it. Rawhide, however, knew what he was about. He was a thrifty one, for he didn't use a stick unless it had first been peeled and the bark eaten. (Poplar bark is the mainstay of a beaver's diet.) Since the peeled sticks were his building material, Rawhide's house went up only as fast as his family could eat.

Rawhide's new construction had taken shape so gradually that when they first went to live in it we were more than surprised that it was actually functioning as a real beaver-house. There was but one difference – unlike the usual structure, this house had an opening leading into our living-room, so the beaver could continue to bring in more mud and sticks (in summer), in case it was necessary to enlarge their living quarters.*

They also used the opening to come for a treat of apples, rice, or whole-wheat bread. Jelly Roll was our most frequent customer; the others, it seemed, were satisfied with their natural diet.

What with Archie at his book, I at my mineralogy studies, and the heavy construction going on below as Rawhide enlarged the house, Beaver Lodge was a going concern.

In the latter part of February all activity came to an abrupt halt – because I had vomited. Archie hovered nearby as I stood over the basin. I wanted to tell him to stay away, but being sick I couldn't talk.

*A beaver enlarges his living space by adding material (mud and sticks) to the outside and then hollowing out the inside as far as the thickness of the structure will allow.

As soon as I could, I gasped out, 'Don't touch me, Archie – don't come near me. Oh, Archie – I've got T.B.!' (After seeing so much T.B. among the Indians, I had a fear of T.B. that amounted to a phobia.) In spite of my efforts to get away, Archie held me tight, trying to calm my fears and comfort me, saying, 'Don't worry, kid, you haven't got T.B. Please believe me, because I know . . . why you'd have had some symptom. . . .'

'That's it!' I interrupted. 'One minute you feel fine, then you get sick, as I did a moment ago, then you go to bed and . . . you're dead.'

'Don't be silly, you're healthy as a horse,' said Archie.

'No, I am not. You just saw me being sick. I might have given it to you . . . maybe the beaver have it too. . . .'

I began to cry and didn't stop till I was exhausted. The same thing happened the next day, so Archie took me as far as Waskesiu where I went by truck to Prince Albert.

The next morning, harried, haggard, and bedraggled, I managed to drag myself off to the sanatorium, where I was X-rayed and examined. After the doctor had studied the X-ray and asked some embarrassing questions, he said that I didn't have T.B., but that I was going to have a baby! Even though I did not grasp the full significance of the doctor's statement, I was stunned at this news, for I had long ago given up all hope of ever having a baby. This is what I had hoped for in the first place, but after six years I had given up the idea – like my dream bungalow in the jackpines. Both had completely faded out of my mind.

When I returned to Ajawaan with the world-shaking news, Archie calmly informed me that he 'kind of thought' that that was my trouble. Why he didn't tell me this, I don't know, but I could have busted him in the head. Anyhow, we were both very happy at the coming event.

Soon we were back to the old routine, Archie working like mad at his paper-cluttered table, and I at mine, which was also cluttered, with mortar and pestle, magnifying glass, books, and some two hundred specimens of rocks and minerals. At this time, I still couldn't believe I was going to have a baby.

The winter passed quickly, but none too soon, for by the time the waters were navigable for canoe, my breeches were too small for me. I had to send for some maternity dresses, but since I hadn't worn a dress in six years, I hadn't a clue as to the size to get; and Archie wasn't much help either, because when I asked him what size I ought to get, he said without hesitation 'Get the biggest!'

Since Beaver Lodge was so far from the hospital, I came in to Prince Albert two weeks before the baby was due. When our daughter was born, on August 23, 1932, I didn't feel that instant love that one hears so much about, when I first held my baby in my arms. My emotion was wonder – the more I looked upon the face of this little stranger, the more I felt that I had known her all my life. Yet, was this wisp of humanity by my side just a figment from one of my wishful dreams, or was she real? I had the fuzzy feeling she had just stopped for a visit and would soon be gone, never to return. When they took her back to the nursery, it was like saying good-bye to my soul – and I cried.

How I longed for Archie to come and share this wonderful miracle with me, but owing to lack of communication, the weather, and a stalled outboard motor, the baby was thirty-six hours old before he was at my side. When he did come, it appeared that his only concern was the state of my health, and when he was satisfied that I was O.K., he then gave a blow-by-blow account of the 102-mile trip from Ajawaan. It was eleven p.m., long after visiting hours, and in the ten minutes he was allowed he hadn't once asked about the baby!

Finally, a nurse came and said that she was sorry, but it was time for Archie to leave. He rose reluctantly, kissed me, and said that he would be back the next afternoon. Bewildered by his lack of interest in our baby, I asked why he didn't want to see her. He was startled at the question and said, 'Oh, I clean forgot. . . . Of course I want to see it.'

I was more than hurt, because he'd forgotten about our daughter, and had called her 'it'. The nurse brought the baby in, and as soon as he saw her he said, 'Holy Mackerel, she looks like a maggot!'

Next day lying in hospital, I was feeling as necessary as a tick on a wooden duck. I waited for what seemed hours for Archie to come to me. I wanted to apologize for being so emotional the day before and also to ask him a million questions, particularly about the cabin the Parks Department was to build and have ready by the time we brought the baby to Ajawaan. But when Archie came with a dozen red roses and with many sweet words, I forgot about the questions, remembering only after the baby was taken back to the nursery.

'Now, tell me all about the new cabin,' I asked.

'Oh yes, the building material is all there, and they're going to start at it in a day or two.'

I was aghast at this bit of news, because I fully intended to go home as soon as I left the hospital. His answer to this was that I couldn't possibly go back until I learned how to take care of 'that' baby. What he said, of course, was true; but I sickened at the thought of going back to that little cubicle where I had waited for two weeks before I came to the hospital. Who was going to teach me child care, I wondered, and how long would it take to learn? Archie rose and went out the door, and he returned immediately with a really chic-looking woman of about thirty-five or forty years of age. She'd apparently been waiting in the hallway for Archie to come for her.

This was the first time I met Mrs. Winters, and I liked her from the very first. It was at the suggestion of Mr. Charlie Walrod, a game-warden friend of ours, that Archie had gone to Mrs. Winters to ask her to teach me baby care.

I won't elaborate on the close relationship that existed between the Winters family and ours, as I will never be able to put into words our deep appreciation for Mrs. Winters' devotion to Shirley Dawn. We have been fast friends for thirty-four years.

I must have thought that babies came equipped with layette, bassinette, etc., for Shirley Dawn didn't have even a diaper she could call her own. My knowledge of the nursery and everything connected with it was negligible, but Mrs. Winters was patient and kind in her endeavour to enlighten me. I don't suppose I would have been so dumb about such things if it hadn't been for the fact that I had just put down my prospector's pick to pick up a safety pin.

It wasn't long till the little 'maggot' had Archie twirling around her little finger. His letters were mainly concerning her welfare – did she remember her Daddy, plans for her future, etc. A father couldn't have loved a child more than Archie did Shirley Dawn.

Finally I had a letter from Archie saying that the cabin was up, but the bunks, tables, benches, etc. still had to be built. He would let me know when all was ready. I thought that since the new cabin was ready, why wait for them to make furniture when there were stores full of it in the city, so I went shopping and ordered a studio lounge, chairs – two big, fat, stuffy ones – material for curtains, a rug, a large mirror, and two tables. I then phoned the Parks' garage in town and asked them to please pick up the furniture and send it right on to Beaver Lodge as soon as possible. I wanted to be sure that the stuff got to Ajawaan before I did, because I didn't want to be there when Archie got the bill.

In the time that we were in Prince Albert, Mrs. Winters had become very attached to the baby and was worried about my taking Dawn so far into the woods to Ajawaan. But when she saw that I was bound to go, she told me that Archie had arranged for a girl to go in with me as a companion. I thought this was the most absurd thing Archie had ever done. Now we'd have to pay her salary, on top of the furniture bill. I was glad that I was nursing the baby, because she, at least, wasn't going to starve.

Hooray! It was a beautiful day, and I was going back home! Alma, my companion, was a good scout, and Shirley Dawn was an angel, so the trip to Beaver Lodge was made without incident – but my home-coming was less of a reunion than it was a surprise party. Since Archie had no idea we were coming, he was properly astonished at our sudden appearance. He was also agitated – if words can describe a man mentally pulling his hair out by the roots; and I too was shocked to a standstill when I saw that the roof was off Beaver Lodge and that the beaver were in a frenzy of activity, which was unusual for that time of day. I sensed that something strange was going on, so I left Archie with his flurry of explanations and ran into the cabin. There, perched atop the bunk, was a photographer taking movies of a procession of beaver carrying sticks and armloads of mud across our living-room floor!

Then I saw the reason for the beaver's feverish labour –

153

their house had been broken open. There was a hole, all of two feet in diameter. I thought that this was going to drastic lengths for the sake of a movie, and I went to Archie and told him so.

'At first I thought the same way too – don't think I didn't,' he said worriedly, and continued, 'That fellow in there is a government photographer, and those films will be shown in schools and God knows where else, so I figured from the conservation angle, the more people know about beaver, the more they will help to save them.'

After the calming effects of a cup of tea, Archie apologized for the none-too-warm reception he had dished out to us on our arrival. His agitation was caused by the fact that they hadn't got around to building the furniture, and, with Beaver Lodge minus a roof, he was worried over the lack of accommodation for Alma and the baby – and the turmoil of movie-making, etc.

There's nothing worse than being caught by unexpected guests with your pants down, unless it is being caught with your roof off.

When it became too dusky for indoor movies, Bill Oliver, the photographer, set his tripod up outside to get more shots of the beaver at work. At the rate they were going, their house would be mended by midnight.

We were sitting around the outdoor fire, watching Bill doing his stuff, when Charlie, our tame moose, came crashing down the hill. It was mating-season (for the moose, not the photographer), and Charlie was on the rampage. He carried on in a most riotous manner, charging the wood-pile with horn and hoof, knocking over the storage tent, and uprooting the saw-horse.

Bill, being the dedicated man that he was, ignored this stomping, snorting moose and kept right on 'shooting' the beaver. Charlie was getting bolder and was edging closer. Archie said we'd better get into the cabin, but Bill paid no heed to the warning. The moose was practically on Bill's back when Archie yelled, 'Bill . . . get the hell in here . . . I warn you I'll not shoot that moose to protect you.'

Bill looked over his shoulder and right into the face of the moose, and simply flew into the cabin, leaving his camera perched on its tripod. Charlie hooked a horn under the whole issue, tossed it into the air, and strode back into the bush. Jelly Roll went to investigate and, finding the loot of great interest, began to drag the camera down to the lake. However, Archie retrieved it in time.

It was dark by the time Archie had a heater set up in the new cabin, where Alma and I slept on the floor and the baby in an 18″ x 30″ packing-box. (The furniture had not yet arrived; in fact, we'd passed it on the Kingsmere portage on our way in.) The next morning Bill and his helper packed their things, and Archie paddled them across to the portage – our gateway to civilization – where, as pre-arranged, he met and brought back the carpenter, who came to fix the roof. Having made the last of several trips to the portage for lumber, Archie began preparations to build the bunks. Of course, I wouldn't let him go on, so squirming inwardly, I went to him and was about to tell him of the furnishings I had bought, when the carpenter shouted from the roof-top, 'Hey, Archie, it looks like somebody is coming up the lake with a piano.' My first thought was that they had sent us a piano by mistake. We hurried to the landing, and there, in the hazy distance, we saw two canoes abreast, with this huge thing straddled across them. Certain now that it was a piano, I said, 'I didn't order that – I got a studio lounge.'

'A studio lounge? What in hell is that?' This from Archie.

'They used to be called a couch or sofa, but this opens out into a bed', I explained.

'It does?' asked Archie doubtfully.

I nodded.

'A double bed?' he asked.

'Yes, nice and wide.'

'Good,' he said.

And that was all there was to it. My burden of guilt evaporated. I really had no reason to have felt as I had, because Archie never did stint on me when there was money to spend. But then this was a big deal, and it was the first time I had ever done anything like it. We weren't exactly rolling in money either.

Now we could see why the couch looked like a piano; there being a fair wind, they had left the back of the studio lounge up, and it was pinch-hitting as a sail.

It was great fun arranging the little cabin with its new splendour, and Archie entered the spirit of the thing, making suggestions as to where this or that piece would look best, admiring the colour scheme, and finally saying we would get some pictures and things for the walls. Little did we know then that in a few short years, people of great importance, some titled, would occupy this cabin as our guests.

When the confusion of the preceding two weeks had come and gone, Archie commenced working on his book again. It had been ten months since he'd started the book, but owing to the continuous interruptions he couldn't have had more than five months' actual work on it; and now that Alma and the baby were with us, there was bound to be more interference. We had neither food nor cooking facilities in the Upper Cabin (as we called the new cabin), so our meals had to be prepared and eaten in Beaver Lodge. This disturbed Archie's sleep. Soon this lack of rest was beginning to tell; he was irritable and unsociable.

One morning Alma came to see me in tears, sobbing something about bacon and ending by saying that Archie was a brute. I dashed down to Archie and asked crossly, 'What's this about the bacon?'

'I've told her again and again that I'm *not* particular about having my bacon crisp,' Archie replied indignantly.

Alma was upset for the rest of the day. When evening came, she asked if she could borrow the canoe. Now Archie would much rather loan his tooth-brush than the canoe, and I was surprised that he consented so cheerfully. I figured that he either wanted to make up for his ill behaviour that morning, or he hoped she'd drown. When eleven p.m. came and Alma hadn't returned, Archie was worried. But since it was dark, there was nothing he could do but wait until daylight to go looking for a capsized canoe. As it turned out, Alma came back at dawn, nursing a hang-over. She'd been at the game warden's on Kingsmere Lake. His cabin was just a short distance from the other end of our portage. Archie was greatly relieved that nothing had happened to her, but he told her, 'I'll arrange as soon as possible for your transportation to Prince Albert – I'm not sending you away on account of your drinking, I do plenty myself. . . .'

So as not to disturb Archie at his writing, or his sleep, I went to his cabin only when it was absolutely necessary. I took to bringing my next day's breakfast and lunch to my cabin and I did the wash only when he was up and around. My day consisted of bringing in the wood and water and taking care of the baby, who was only two months old and slept most of the time. After the baby came, I figured that my prospecting days were over, so I put my rocks aside – studying mineralogy now would be like knitting by day and unravelling by night. In other words, I had time on my hands, which I wished I hadn't. I began to dislike the cabin more and more. It was like living in a hotel room. Even Archie said, 'Every time I come up here, I keep looking at the door, expecting the hostess to come in. This just doesn't feel like our place.'

So right after Ajawaan froze over and the beaver went to their quarters for the winter, we scrubbed Beaver Lodge from top to bottom, brought the curtains, a stuffed chair, and the rug down from the Upper Cabin, and covered the beaver-house with a tarpaulin to keep the dust down. Then the baby and I moved in. After her third month Shirley Dawn grew more interesting each day and would entertain us by the hour. At seven months she was 'real people'.

Winter came and went, and soon break-up was upon us. This, at a certain stage, makes it impossible to travel in the north. We thought it wise, in case of illness, to take the baby into town while the ice was still firm enough to carry us. The warm April sun makes heavy snowshoeing so we waited for the night frost to tighten up the soggy snow before we started for Waskesiu. Archie laughed because I insisted on carrying the rifle for fear of a wolf pack attacking us and eating up the baby. In all my travels in the woods I had never given wolves so much as a thought, but now here I was following the toboggan with bristling hair and straining eyes, imagining a wolf in every shadow. Every few minutes I'd ask Archie to stop so I could wriggle my hand under the toboggan sheet, blankets, and the robe, to see if the baby was warm enough. She always was, and so she should have been, because she was in a rabbit robe that I had won in a hot game of poker from a Hudson's Bay factor out north. Archie saw us off to Prince Albert and returned to Ajawaan. We, of course, stayed at the Winters'.

Shirley Dawn was nine months old when I received a wire from a prospector whom I'd met at Elk Lake, advising me to hurry down to Chapleau, Ontario and do some staking at a new discovery there. This would take about a month, including travelling time. I asked Mrs. Winters if she would take care of Dawn while I was away. She said that she'd be glad to do so, and I left for Chapleau as soon as it could be arranged between Archie and me.

When I arrived at Chapleau, I was prevented from going into the woods by a drenching rain. I had never been away from Dawn for even an hour since we'd left the hospital after her birth, and I thought I'd die with longing for her. It rained for five whole days and nights, and all I did during that time was play the 'Blue Danube' and 'Ave Maria' over and over and think of the baby. At last I could stand it no longer, so I took the first westbound train and counted the seconds till I had Dawn in my arms again.

My prospector had given me a genuine tip, for that discovery is now either Halcrow or the Wright-Hargreaves mines (I've forgotten which). Then, within a month, I received another letter from a prospector who was then at Great Bear Lake in the Arctic, where Gilbert LaBine had discovered the biggest body of pitchblende (a radium ore) in the world. The letter said, in effect, 'Come immediately and help blanket the country [claim-staking with abandon], and join the big doings up here.'

In spite of the first fiasco, I was triggered to go again. This time I would know just how dreadful a thing this yearning for my baby could be. I would not be taken unawares as I was on that trip to Chapleau and, therefore, would be able to fight it.

There was, however, a $5,000 obstacle in the way of getting to Great Bear. One had to have a return ticket by plane from Edmonton, Alberta to the Arctic, proper equipment and clothing, and sufficient provisions. The Mounties were there to see that you weren't going to be a drag on the country. I knew that we didn't have anywhere near $5,000, but that didn't daunt this eager beaver. I went to Ajawaan and showed Archie the letter. (I had kept in touch with four or five prospectors. At first Archie didn't appreciate my writing to them, and once he asked, 'Don't you think I ever get jealous?' I thought the question so ridiculous that it didn't rate an answer. After Archie began adding postscripts to my letters to them, they started addressing their letters to the both of us.) I asked Archie if he could possibly get me a one-way ticket to Toronto, where I knew three mining men, who, I figured, would grubstake me to Great Bear Lake. He said he would manage it, somehow, and he did, but he insisted that I get a return ticket, just in case.

In Toronto I could locate only one of the three men I had come to see, a Mr. Jowsey. The others were away – to the Great Bear, where else? Mr. Jowsey was a brother of the prospector whose outfit I had taken to the half-way the time lightning had struck my camp. When I told him what I wanted he said, 'I've heard a lot about you – after all, you are the only lone "she" prospector in the country – and I know you're capable of taking care of yourself in the bush; but I would stop you if I could, rather than help you to go into that country.' We had lunch together, but no amount of coaxing would change his mind.

I was determined not to go back home empty-handed, so I decided to go to Buffalo, New York, to see a Mr. Wetlauffer, whom I'd met in the Elk Lake country when he was on a holiday canoe trip. His attitude towards my going into the Arctic was comparable to Mr. Jowsey's.

'Fine,' he said. 'Sure I'll stake you to $5,000, but not to go into that God-forsaken land. Why the very thought that I was responsible for sending a girl there would drive me nuts. If you are bound to go prospecting, why not try Ontario?'

Why not? Simply because if you are prospecting, unless you make a strike, you are in the bush till freeze-up forces you to quit, whereas with claim-staking you are there only as long as it takes to cut the lines.

So this, too, was a fizzle – I didn't get to Great Bear. Indeed, I counted my lucky stars that I got home at all, for I had spent my 'eating money' on the wild-goose chase to Buffalo.

Dawn and I spent the rest of that summer at Beaver Lodge, but with Archie being so wrapped up in his writing I found Ajawaan indescribably dull and decided to spend the winter in Prince Albert, where there would be some diversion, and people to talk with. But then, even though the Winters' family were always more than kind and wonderful to us, boarding out wasn't exactly a satisfactory way of life either.

Archie saw us off to Prince Albert in the game warden's

canoe. As we left, I could see him standing on shore, watching us; I looked back till his outline faded and merged with the trees. Archie was a lonely man.

It was a dull, bleak morning, reflecting my mood exactly, and as the miles separated us from Beaver Lodge, my thoughts went back to the time, in the Jumping Caribou country, when I had longed so terribly for a baby and a place we could call our own; and I remembered how hurt I had been when Archie said 'No. No babies,' and insisted that a permanent establishment suffocated him.

Now I had two homes at Ajawaan, and I found neither joy or contentment in either of them; I had the baby I had wanted so badly, whom I loved more than anything in the world, yet I had to fight an urge, almost unbearable at times, to go north again. Was I abnormal? I thought I was and worried till I was a nervous wreck – this is no exaggeration. The expression 'the call of the wild' is hackneyed and a joke with most people, but with me it was a disease, and by spring, 1934, I knew I would have to make one more trip – out there.

⁄•\⁄•\⁄•\⁄•\

Having made up my mind, I decided to go to God's Lake, 400 miles as the crow flies – I couldn't begin to guess how many miles it was by water. Since I feared that Archie wouldn't understand what this trip meant to me, I didn't intend to tell him of my plans until I was well on the way, so I couldn't go to Ajawaan to get my outfit without offering some explanation. However, the problem was soon solved – I went to a hardware store and asked if our credit was good. Upon finding that it was, I ordered an axe, cooking-utensils, tent, mosquito bar, sleeping-bag, rifle, dynamite, prospector's pick, and a prospector's license. When I got through shopping, Archie owed about $900 – and things were dirt cheap in those days too.

For fear of a hitch that might prevent me from going, I made arrangements with the Winters to care for Dawn, and I lost no time in getting on with the journey. I launched my canoe into Waskesiu Lake the very next day. To begin with, there was forty-five miles of shallow rapids. To avoid ripping the canoe on the rocks because of a too-heavy load, I had to wade, and guide the craft down the swift water rather than check it with a pole.

As careful as I'd been (I'd even pondered over the weight of my reading matter, which was Shakespeare and the Bible – that quantity of reading, in any other form, would sink a ship), I had miscalculated the capacity of the sixteen-foot canoe. I was tempted to jettison some of the load, but didn't have the courage.

However, I soon got rid of the surplus by getting in a poker game with the Cree women at Montreal Lake. Instead of putting up the money, I'd throw anything from a bar of soap to a bag of beans onto the gaming blanket, while they would wager buckskin mitts, moccasins, beaded belts, snuff, etc. – these gals loved their snuff and poker. Montreal Lake is at the end of the rapids, forty-five miles from Waskesiu. I wrote to Archie from there.

The next lap of the trip was to Lac la Ronge, eighty miles north. To keep my mind from dwelling on my loneliness for Shirley Dawn, I travelled my every waking hour and was often too tired to put up the tent at night. As soon as my eyes were opened, I would be gone again. Rain or shine I kept going, and that's why I arrived at Lac la Ronge soaked to the marrow.

Fortunately, I had a letter of introduction to a couple of prospectors there. Bill Wright, who gave me the letter, told me to be sure and go see them because they were 'a couple of good fellows'. They were good fellows. When Tremblay saw my soggy condition, he rushed me to the house and introduced me to his wife, who soon had me dried out and fed.

I was fortunate; I hit Lac la Ronge on a night of 'goings-on'. There was a wedding dance, but there seemed to be some problem. The plane wasn't able to come in because of bad weather, and there wouldn't be a drop to drink. However, while we were pondering this catastrophe, Ole's face brightened and he said, 'I just thought of something. The fire-ranger said that if he wasn't here, I could go over and use up his batch of brew before it turned to vinegar.'

So, after dark, with our pots – big ones – we went to the fire-ranger's warehouse. We'd no sooner started straining the stuff than we heard the door softly open. Ole snapped off the flashlight; we ran for cover behind a gasoline drum and waited, and who do you suppose came tiptoeing towards the brew? None other than the Mountie who was stationed here, and he had a pot too. Scarcely above a whisper, Ole said the Mountie's name and then gave his own. We all had a good laugh.

There was a letter from Archie at Lac la Ronge. I remember that half of the first page was taken up with the drawing of a scowling, fanged owl. This was followed by a row of corkscrews, stars, lightning, etc., punctuated by exclamation marks, and then he wrote:

> No, I'm not mad at you Gurdy, I only envy you. I'm so balled up and tied up with this god-damned sitting on my ass writing – I've lost any gumption that I ever had – I feel so useless I think I would be satisfied if all I could do is carry the tea-pail and the tomahawk over the portages, just to be on a trip like yours. I am proud of you for having the courage to take on a trip like that. [Courage? They couldn't have held me back with a logging chain.] This is a case of the student overtaking the master.

The next trading post was Fort Stanley, about eighty miles north of La Ronge, on the Churchill River, which falls into Hudson Bay. When I got there I met a young Indian and his wife, and when the husband discovered that I was interested in prospecting, he told me he had found some nice shiny stones and he would take me to the spot if I wanted to go. We left immediately. Though we were travelling light and had an outboard motor, it took us five days to get to our destination, which was north of Wollaston Lake on the edge of the Barren Lands. When we got there, they showed me an outcropping of iron pyrite. I looked the country over for a couple of days and figured that it wasn't worth staking. I was looking for gold.

I had no intention whatsoever of going to Reindeer Lake, seventy or eighty miles north, but I just happened to be camping at an old and much-used campsite when along came two families of Cree Indians from Fort Stanley who were bound for Lac du Brochet, a trading post and an Indian summerplace north of Reindeer Lake, to visit with relatives. They had heard of a lone woman-traveller; therefore they knew im-

162

mediately who I was and were most friendly. Indians are shy when it comes to enquiring into other people's business; however, the question as to where I was going was finally asked. I took out my map and pointed to God's Lake, Manitoba, which happened to be some distance away, like six hundred miles. The chief shook his head incredulously and asked 'Why?' I said that I just wanted to see a whole bunch of country. They talked among themselves a bit, and then I was invited to go north with them. Women don't travel alone in that country, and I could see that they were concerned over my welfare. I appreciated this, and since they had two outboard motors – well, it was like being invited to hop into a Cadillac when one has been pushing a wheelbarrow – so I accepted.

Next morning, because I was going to travel light, the men hoisted most of my stuff onto an ancient cache. (An elevated cache is a storage platform not less than nine feet high, with legs consisting of four sturdy posts planted in the ground. The top extends three feet out from the props in order to prevent porcupines, bears, wolverines, etc. from climbing over the edge and getting into the provisions.) When the canoes were loaded and we were about to embark, I noticed that my canoe was not hitched for towing. Upon enquiring about it, I was told that my canoe was on a rack, and it would be safe till we got back. In other words, I was to spend the summer with them! However, I needed the canoe, for I intended to make only a quick trip to Reindeer and back with them, and then get on with my journey. The canoe was hitched up only after I said, 'I promise, as soon as I get back to the Churchill River, I will go straight home to my husband and to hell with God's Lake.'

They were the most enjoyable travelling companions that I had ever been with; no hustle, no bustle; one had only to throw out a troll and there was a fish! We had bannock, pemmican, fish and tea galore throughout the long leisurely cruise up the river. At last we arrived at the lake.

Reindeer Lake is 150 miles from the south to the north end. It was too large a lake for me and my little six-footer. So I bade my friends a fond farewell. I had gone up the river in a motor-driven craft and I didn't realize how swift the current really was, so my trip back was fast and furious. I was alone once again and more lonesome than ever for Dawn, and I guess that was my reason for deciding it was too late in the summer to go on to God's Lake after all. I took a water route to the nearest railroad, which was at Flin Flon, a Manitoba mining town. At last the canoe was pointing southward, and I was happy, because Shirley Dawn was in that direction and I would soon be with her.

On the way to Flin Flon I had a chance to send a letter off to Archie by plane, from Pelican Narrows. In this letter I told him that I was on my way back to Prince Albert.

It took about ten days' paddling before I got to the next community. I hadn't seen so many people in one place at one time since I had left Waskesiu three months before. There were two stores, a fish camp, a mink farm, and a freighting company. I landed at Amisk Lake, nineteen miles from Flin Flon. There was a claim-staking spree going on at Amisk Island, three miles to the south-west side of the lake. I met Eric Erickson, the man who made the discovery (it's been so long since then, that I have forgotten what the find was), and he told me that there was still some open ground on the island and that it would be worth my while to do some staking, but I was more interested in getting back to Shirley Dawn. So I went to Flin Flon, where I expected to get a letter and money for my fare to Prince Albert. I got the letter all right. It read:

Dear Gurdy, Your letter surprised me. After all, you've written only twice in five months. . . . Since you left without telling me that you were going, I should think that you'd have the grace to *ask* if you could come back . . . instead of telling me that you were. . . . I, too, would like nothing better than to drop everything and take off . . . but I have my responsibilities, and must face them, and I expect you to do the same. What I mean is, you've got to look after yourself, at least till I can catch up on my bills. . . . Your coming and going as you see fit puts me in an awkward position. I know exactly what they are thinking of me. . . . I used to think the same of John. His wife was an actress, who spent most of her time in New York, but she'd come and see John every once in a while, either between shows or to get her strength back (after all that city life). Anyway, we used to think that John was a sucker.

After I tore up Archie's letter, I went to the recording office for a prospector's license, returned to Amisk, and looked up Eric. When I found him, he showed me on a blueprint where to stake.

I made camp on a wide, flat rock – a natural patio. It was bare as a billiard ball and a difficult place to set up a tent, but it had a wonderful view of the lake and surrounding country. Its other redeeming factor was a pot-hole at the edge of the lake where the slightest breeze changed the water – it was Mother Nature's own bathtub. What it lacked in privacy it made up in convenience. I just kept my eyes open.

By the time the staking was finished, and that means cutting brush and lots of it, October was on its last legs and freeze-up was just around the corner. I made a rush trip to the mining town to record my three claims and then went looking for work. Of course that was a laugh – there was a depression on. My only opening now was to go to The Pas, sixty miles east of Amisk Lake, down the Sturgeon River, and if I couldn't get work there, I would have to sell the canoe for a ticket to Prince Albert.

It isn't any wonder the canoe was overloaded when I started out from Waskesiu, for I still had plenty of dehydrated fruit and vegetables, sow-belly, beans, etc. Of course, I had a lot of fish on the trip and had got pemmican from Fort Stanley, Pelican Narrows, and from the odd Indian family that I'd met, which was a great saving on my stock of provisions. Actually, the larder was short of only a few items, so I sold the rifle to purchase what was necessary and returned to Amisk. But I couldn't get on with the journey for ten whole days on account of wind and rain. At last, when the weather settled, I stepped into the canoe. I should say staggered into the canoe, because I was as sick as a dog.

After twenty-two miles I came to the head of the Sturgeon Weir River, where there was a group of old log buildings. Amidst a pack of barking dogs stood a man, beckoning to me. Paddling to the landing I recognized Angus McDonald, whom I'd met but once before. When I told him where I was off to, he was surprised.

'Boy, you're cutting it pretty fine. Cranberry Lake, below

here, is very shallow and it freezes over in no time. It's getting late in the day – you better stay in for the night, and I'll take you down four or five rapids in the morning.'

'No, thank you,' I said, 'I'd better keep going till dark.'

'Well, come in for a dish of tea anyway.'

I couldn't resist that. When I disembarked, he pointed to a building and said, 'You go up there and put the tea-pail on. I'll be with you in a minute.'

When I walked into the place, I felt sure that I'd made a mistake and had gone into the wrong house, because no one, I thought, could possibly live in such a mess. The table, benches, floor – everything – was caked with dirt. There was a bunk – actually two bunks, for it was the length of the building. I sat and waited for Angus to take me to his living-quarters. It was only when he came in and said, 'Oh, you didn't put on the tea-pail,' that I knew definitely he lived there.

Even though the top end of the bunk was heaped with traps, haywire, several lengths of stove-pipe, a chunk of moose-hide, etc., it began to look more inviting as the minutes passed, so, at last I asked, 'Would you mind if I lie down until the tea is ready? I don't feel well.'

'I kinda thought you didn't look good – your face is all red,' said Angus as he cleared off the bunk. I went to it, and I remember no more.

When I awakened, Angus was sitting by my bed, anxious eyes staring from his worried face. I said, 'I'm sorry. I guess I went to sleep. . . .'

'Sleep nothing. I thought you were dead!'

I chuckled thinly, thinking he was making a joke, but when I noticed that I was in my sleeping-bag and unable to get up, I realized that it was no joke. I'd been unconscious for three days.

Now Angus was clucking about like a mother hen. Every time I closed my eyes he'd be there, asking anxiously if I were awake. He made tea, he made cocoa, and he warmed up a pot of wild-goose broth. He was disappointed when I said all I wanted was a cold drink of water.

'Then' he said, 'I'll make you a nice raisin pie. . . .' Oh, my stomach. In spite of my protests, he went ahead with it – bannock dough and raisins – very heavy and soggy.

I was fully dressed, except for my boots and jacket, and wanting to go to the 'bathroom'. I struggled to get out of bed.

'Now, what do you think you're doing?' queried Angus reproachfully.

'I've got to go outside. . . .'

'No, no. Here's a lard pail – been keeping it handy. . . . I'd better go and see about the dogs. . . .'

Angus' place was known as the 'half-way' in the days before the railroad was built between The Pas and Flin Flon. All the machinery and supplies for the mining community had to pass through here on 'swings' (horse and sleigh). Angus, in telling the story of how he got into the 'hotel' business, said, 'Them freighters were too damn lazy to make their own camp, so they used to come and stay here overnight. Sometimes this shack was so crowded you couldn't walk across the floor without stepping on somebody. So, I built a stable – my, I used to feel sorry for the horses, out there in the cold nights. I had plenty of hay for them too, but I told the freighters if they didn't want to get poisoned, they'd better bring their own grub.'

After the railroad put him out of business, Angus remained at the old place. He was trapping when I was there.

By the time I was strong enough to paddle, pack over portages, and handle a canoe in white water, my route to The Pas was blocked by ice on Cranberry Lake, so I could only wait till Amisk froze over, when I would be able to go to Flin Flon and on to Prince Albert from there.

Angus had a heart of gold, but he just didn't know the meaning of the word 'cleanliness'. I was horrified when he came in one day with a load of fish and began chopping them up for dog food right in the middle of the floor.

'Angus!' was all I could say.

'Oh, excuse me – I forgot that somebody was here.'

Another time, as soon as I got out of bed, I began to wash the walls, against his wild protests. Being still weak and dizzy, I nearly fell off a bench. Angus got excited and shouted, 'You see! You're going to kill yourself yet. You don't have to do that – nobody's coming here till next spring.'

I was standing over him, pouring tea, when I noticed that his head was black with dirt. He'd remarked a couple of times that his head was 'full of bumps'. Now I knew why, but how was I going to get him to shampoo? I had an idea, and that night I rubbed olive oil in my scalp and kept it up till he asked what I was doing. I told him that a person would never go bald if he did what I was doing every once in a while, and asked if he would like to try some. He did, and after he was well saturated with oil, I said he would have to wash it off; otherwise, it would burn his hair. He did and after the shampoo he looked into the mirror and roared, 'I'm bald, I'm bald. ... That stuff took all the hair off!' I shook my head. His eyes widened, and he asked, 'Them bumps on my head – was dirt?'

'Yes,' I replied.

He wagged his head sadly, saying, 'How can a man get so dirty?'

Then he told me of a fellow he used to laugh at, because the man never took off socks or underwear once he had put them on – he'd just pull new ones on over the old ones. Not believing this, I said, 'In that case, he must have gone about with dozens and dozens of underwear. ...'

'No, they just flew away in dust.'

Archie hadn't a clue as to where I was; Angus knew this and insisted that I write to him and he would see that it was mailed. When I told Angus I was never going to write to Archie again, he took my arm gently but firmly, sat me before a writing-pad, and said, 'Now, write that letter.'

'I'll write if you'll write,' I said, thinking that that would stop him, but it didn't. He said 'O.K., I'll do it,' and he rolled up his sleeves, washed his hands and face, rubbed some grease from the fry-pan on his head, then sat before the writing-pad and said 'Jesus'. Then he wrote the letter. We had to walk twenty-nine miles through the bush to Cranberry Portage, the closest post office, to mail the letters.

Amisk, being a large lake, didn't freeze over till the first week in December. In the meantime, Angus went on with the mink hunt, and, the weather not being cold enough to keep fresh meat, I smoked and cured the moose, Canadian geese, and ducks that Angus had shot. And I also tended the fish-net and fed the dogs – nineteen of them! Though a trapper, Angus couldn't kill a dog; consequently, he had to fish and hunt continuously to feed them.

Before Amisk was completely frozen over, I could have gone out to Flin Flon by walking the shore, but if I had, Angus would have insisted on taking me out. Since I didn't want to interfere with the mink hunt, I waited for the ice and for Angus to catch, as he put it, 'that stubborn coyote'. This coyote evidently refused to go near the traps. Angus, mystified, said, 'I can't understand why he doesn't get into them – I've got bait that stinks enough to knock a dog off a gut-wagon.'

Instead of selling my canoe to Angus, I would have loved to have given it to him for all the kindness he'd shown me, but I had to have the money for the fare to Prince Albert. Christmas week, Angus harnessed up the dogs and away we went to Flin Flon.

The first thing we did when we got to town was to engage rooms; then Angus contacted a fur-buyer who happened to be in the same hotel, and I went to the post office. There was a parcel and three letters, one from Archie, the others from Mrs. Winters. Knowing that at least I would hear all about Shirley Dawn, who was staying with the Winters in my absence, I wanted to read the letters in the peace and quiet of my room. I made a mad dash to the hotel, my heart bursting – I was going to spend Christmas with my daughter.

The letters said that my daughter was well and happy, and among the pages was a sheet covered with X's (kisses) scribbled by Shirley Dawn. The parcel contained gifts, including Christmas pudding and cake from the Winters.

As I was opening Archie's letter, Angus came in and just at an opportune moment – there was a letter enclosed for him. Angus' pleasure at receiving Archie's letter was pathetic, and he insisted that I read it to him. Archie expressed his appreciation to Angus for his kindness to me, especially when I had been ill. There was a Christmas gift of five dollars and an invitation to Beaver Lodge in the summer.

Archie's letter to me was long, sad, and reminiscent. He wrote of McGinty and McGinnis, Hingy and Papati; of past happenings – how we'd reacted at this or that place, what we'd said at such and such a time, etc. I also received a gift of twenty-five dollars, but there was no invitation to return home. I decided then and there that I would never go back unless this invitation was extended. So I wasn't to be with Dawn for Christmas after all.

Overwhelmed with self-pity, I guess I went a little haywire and drank too much. By the time Christmas had gone, so had my money, including what I'd got for the canoe. This was the end. I would walk till I dropped and froze to death. The depression had brought many people to jump from windows, etc., but I didn't have a window high enough.

Once my mind was made up, I ran to Angus' room and told him that I had to leave in a hurry, but that I would write him as soon as I got there.

'Where?' he interrupted, his eyes penetrating.

'That's a secret,' I answered flippantly.

'It ain't the secret you think it is – and I'm going to follow you.'

'Don't be silly, Angus,' I said, getting angry.

'When you walk out the door, I'll walk too,' he said quietly, and I knew he meant it.

'O.K. . . but right now I'm going to have a little rest. . . I don't feel so good. . . . I'll let you know when I'm leaving,' I said, hoping to give him the slip. He walked me to my door and must have stood guard there in the hallway, for every time I attempted to leave, there he'd be. At last he came in, sat down, and began to talk. He said, 'I like you just as my own daughter. . . .You have helped me by showing me how to live like a human being again. Now, what can I do to help you?'

I thanked him, but there was nothing he could do.

'The thing I want you to do is to come back to Sturgeon Weir. I want to take care of you until your mind gets straightened out,' he said. I was close to tears. 'C'mon, cheer up,' he coaxed. 'You have nothing to worry about. Course, I know only too well how you're feeling. When I was young I used to go to The Pas – that was a wild town – and many's the time I pulled out of there wishing I'd fall through the ice before I got back to camp, and never come up again. But as soon as I got a lung full of fresh, clean air and lots to eat, my worries passed, and I felt like a new man again. So pack up, and let's go.'

Yes, why not? I was waiting in front of the hotel when Angus came around with the dogs. As I stepped into the carriole I asked, 'Is The Pas as good as Flin Flon for being bad?'

'Yes, worse.'

We arrived at Amisk after dark, so we went to stay for the night with Andrew, one of the old-timers who came to visit me when I was camped on 'the Rock'. We'd no sooner offered each other the season's greetings than a woman named Helen Chatten called. The first thing she said was that she had been trying to get in touch with me, because she wanted someone to stay with her. Her husband, a miner, came home only every other weekend, and she didn't like being alone. Now I had a job as companion, at twelve dollars a month – whee! All joking aside, I was glad of it.

Helen had a great team of dogs, so when George, her husband, came home every other weekend, I'd take the dogs and go down to see Angus. Between flying around the lake with the dogs, visiting, and playing cribbage, the winter passed.

For Mother's Day, Archie wired a bouquet of red roses. Of course, being thirty-five miles in the bush, I didn't get them on the exact day. However, I wrote the florist in Flin Flon saying that I would collect the roses when I came to town.

In June Helen went to live in town with George, and I sold my claims for $300 and went prospecting.

In August, anxious to get news of Shirley Dawn, I made a rush trip out to Amisk Lake, and this was when I received a letter from Archie, telling me he was going to England on a lecture tour and asking me to come home. This was what I'd been waiting for – the invitation – no matter how often I had longed to go home. (I never would have gone till I was asked.) Call it stubbornness; Archie called it stinking pride.

Before leaving for Prince Albert, I had to go back for my outfit. Then I went to see Angus. He was happy for me, and I was happy too when he told me that he was going to Saskatchewan to live the rest of his days with his brother.

Mrs. Winters brought Shirley Dawn to the station to meet me. While they waited for me to disembark, Mrs. Winters pointed to a woman, who'd got off the train ahead of me, and she said to Shirley Dawn, 'There's your mother!' Shirley Dawn said, 'No, dat's not my mudder!' After a whole year, she remembered!

171

We had a grand and glorious reunion, Shirley Dawn and I. I hoped never to leave her again, but as luck would have it, just as we were to leave for Beaver Lodge I received word from Archie saying that he was due to sail for England a month earlier than expected; and not to bring the baby because there was so much to do we would be unable to give her the necessary attention. So the baby and I had but one precious week together, and then I had to go to Ajawaan, where I would remain until Archie returned from England, in the spring.

It wasn't exactly an ideal homecoming, for Archie was in a state of nerves. He'd been hoping for a month's delay of the trip and hadn't got down to writing his lectures. So now, with a month less to do it, he was up to his ears in a frenzy of work. He also suffered from great doubts as to his ability to face an audience, to lecture on such a grand scale. He was afraid of letting them down, and with them, the 'little people' whose cause he was going to plead. But he realized that if ever there was a chance of getting across to the public his conservation ideas, this was it, and he said he was going to do it if he died in the attempt.

Archie opened the mail that I had brought in and discovered a clipping in one of the letters. The clipping was from some publication, and upon reading it Archie banged the table with a clenched fist, got up and circled the room in a rage.

'I was afraid of – this!' he hissed, handing me the clipping.

It was a sweet piece of work. It said that Archie was the saviour of the animal kingdom and likened him to St. Francis of Assisi. I liked it and couldn't see what upset him so. Besides, St. Francis was a favourite saint of mine. I used to pray to him for help in finding lost articles, such as socks, garters, shoes, etc. I asked Archie what he was so steamed up about.

'Can't you see what they're trying to do?'

'Who's trying to do what?' I wanted to know.

'The kind of people who write such things. Just because I'm trying to make up for some of the suffering I've caused in my day, they're making me out to be some kind of evangelist – a saint . . . me? Huh, that is funny. I'm one of the worst bastards that ever walked. Poor ol' St. Francis – he must have flipped in his crypt.'

The next morning Archie went, by plane, to Lac la Ronge

for the buckskin that I was to make into a hunting shirt and leggings for him. For a man who hated heights as Archie did, flying was an ordeal. On his return he told me that to feel a 'smidgen' of security on the flight, he'd held to a rope so tightly that his hands cramped. When they had landed, the pilot had said, 'Hey Archie, were you scared that in case of engine failure you wouldn't get down? That was the anchor-line you were holding.'

Archie brought back five moose-hides and about two pounds of beads, but since every stitch of his outfit had to be hand-sewn, with only three weeks to do it in, I told him that I wouldn't have time for beadwork – and besides all that fancy stuff would make him look sissified.

To this he answered, 'Do Indians in full regalia look sissified?'

'No, but a bushman would look funny all decorated up.'

'I agree with you there. But I'm not going as a bushman, I'm going as the Indian they expect me to be.'

'Archie!' I said aghast.

'Read the fan mail and the book reviews, and you'll see what I mean. And besides, in case I can't deliver the goods, I can at least give them a show for their money.'

'But Archie, you can't!'

'Maybe not, but I'd do anything, and I mean *anything,* if I thought it would make people listen to what I've got to say.' I remained silent. Then he said, 'Don't worry, kid. When I step down, they'll forget all about me, my feathers, beads and buck-skin, but in the meantime, I'll have – or I'll hope to have – sown a seed or two that'll make people realize that we've got to save the bush and everything in it – and it's got to start right now, not tomorrow. It will be too late then.'

Archie made the beadwork designs for his buckskin shirt and leggings, and after my screaming objections to beadwork, once I got started I got carried away and put a maple leaf for Canada on one shoulder, and a white beaver, for luck, on the other. So, literally speaking, I was beading up to the hour he left.

Everything was ready to go; that is, everything but Archie, but the journey could not be put off any longer. He said he would not go at all if there was any other way of bringing understanding to the people. He did not appear the crusader or

173

a St. Francis on a pilgrimage as he started towards the canoe; his expression was one of naked fear, saved only from indignity by a forced, broad smile, which was quickly fading into a grimace.

As the canoe slowly slid out into Lake Ajawaan, he turned and waved. Although still not too far from shore, his voice was almost inaudible as he said, 'Well, England, here I come' – a lone envoy from the wilds of Canada, in a canoe, on the first leg of a 7,500-mile journey. He turned his back to Beaver Lodge, and with the sure, strong stroke of his paddle, the canoe lept forward – to what? Success or failure?

For the younger generation, and for those who may not have heard of Grey Owl, I am including clippings that refer to the success of the tour.

> A new Canadian ambassador [Grey Owl] is taking London – and all England for that matter – by storm.

> Grey Owl, the Canadian Indian who has established world fame for himself as conservator of game and as a modern Hiawatha, is paying a visit to this country and has already broadcast from the B.B.C. His reputation has preceded him through his books, and he proudly numbers the King and Queen among those who possess the stories he has written of the beavers and the animals of the Wilds.

> Arthur Leslie of the Polytechnic Cinema tells me that the Grey Owl film lectures, which were sponsored recently at the theatre, were among the most popular programmes he ever put on.

> Today Grey Owl is one of the most sought-after lecturers alive.

> Sir John Lavery is busy putting the finishing touches on his portraits of Lady Simon and Grey Owl, ready for their inclusion in the next academy show.

'I only seek in this work to lay a foundation on which abler hands and wiser heads may later build,' Grey Owl told his audience during the tour.

Shirley Dawn was in hospital with pneumonia when Archie re-

Grey Owl with Indians

The Hotel Senneterre in northern Quebec was a gathering place
for trappers each spring.

Anahareo talks with beaver.

Dave

Anahareo with Dawn at Lake
Ajawaan, 1935

Hudson's Bay Company store at Biscotasing, where Archie went often
between 1906 and 1914.

Anahareo with Dawn, probably in the late 1930's.

Archie's aunts Ada and Carrie, probably around 1900.

turned from England and the tour, and as soon as Dawn recovered, he went home to Beaver Lodge. After the solitary winter at Ajawaan, I was in no hurry to return to Beaver Lodge, so Dawn and I spent the summer at Waskesiu. I saw very little of Archie till September, when a most unfortunate accident occurred. The accident came about while I was on a trip with Professor Cocherel, an entomologist from Colorado, and his wife. I saw a friend, a Parks warden, drown. I phoned Archie as soon as I possibly could. He'd already heard. I was terribly upset, so he told me to come immediately, with Dawn, to Beaver Lodge. We arrived the fourth of September, two days later.

I don't know when it began, but Archie and I had grown pretty far apart. I guess he saw the writing on the wall long before I did, because several times when I was planning on a trip, I remember Archie saying, 'The only way I can hold you . . . is by letting you go.'

However, we thought, or hoped, that it wasn't too late to bridge the chasm between us, and we earnestly tried to recapture the spirit that had, in the past, held us together through thick and thin. But Archie was in the midst of writing *Tales of an Empty Cabin,* so except for time out to play with Shirley Dawn, seeing the beaver, and eating, he was always busy. After two months of this, I despaired, for I knew that I could not live at Ajawaan. Perhaps if I had been a little older (there was a difference of over eighteen years between Archie's age and mine), I might have been quite content to remain there, but I wasn't. Archie knew this and was sympathetic. One night, his face taking on that same expression as when he spoke of war or Aunt Ada, he said, 'I know how you feel about this continuous preoccupation of mine . . . and I could promise you that the next book, which I must write, will be my last, but I don't need to . . . because once they've read *The Devil in Deer-skins* – that's what I'm going to call it – they'll never read another line from me. . . .'

'Then why write it?' I asked.

'Because I've got to. I owe that much to you, to Shirley Dawn, the beaver, and everyone concerned. Do you know that it wasn't till I was over there [England] that I realized how sincere and genuine people really are?' He paused, then added, 'I suppose I was sceptical on account of my Aunt.'

It had become second nature to change the subject as soon as Aunt Ada was mentioned, so I asked jokingly, 'What's the book going to be about – A ghost story about a hen?'

'I wish it were that simple. No, it's about me – things that even you don't know, and will never know; at least, not from me. . . .'

'So, I'm to be the only one that's not going to read the book?'

'It won't be published until I'm dead.'

We did not succeed, as we'd hoped, in bridging the gap between us, and so we parted. Before leaving, I told Archie, as I always had, that if ever he needed me, to send for me. To this he answered, 'Thanks, kid, I appreciate that very much. And remember this – I won't forget you in my will.'

'Oh, quit talking like that!' I said sharply.

'Why? I'm not going to live forever. . . .'

I left Beaver Lodge, for the last time, on November 15, 1936.

Epilogue

After his *Tales of an Empty Cabin* was published, Archie was again asked to lecture in England. That tour, too, was a success, in that people were becoming more aware of the plight of the Indian, the probable extinction of the beaver, the callous brutality towards animals, and the wholesale slaughter of our forests, of which Archie sadly wrote: 'The soughing of the Wind in the trees, as though the forest [were] sighing – praying to be spared. . . .' He also said:

The commercial instincts of man are often stronger than his humanity, even in respect of his own kind, let alone an animal. Given the opportunity, with the present day attitude toward beaver, man will kill them out to the last one. The moment a beaver allows a peeled stick to show where a passer-by may see it, he and his entire family are doomed. Those within the National Parks are safe, but in time these will overflow the boundaries, and if a moiety of these are to be saved to fulfill the purpose for which they were intended, there must be a radical change in man's attitude towards them, and this cannot be brought about by coercion.

No body of armed men could successfully police the Northern wastes. No democratic race of people can be legislated into a state of mind, whether it be on religion or conservation. Education of the public through the appeal to their sense of justice and economy, giving them a thorough knowledge of the subject in hand by means of lectures, writings, moving pictures, and actual demonstrations, will accomplish more in one season than the most harshly enforced laws would ever do.

On April 13, 1938, the black headlines read: 'End Comes for Grey Owl at 8:30 This Morning. Succumbs to Pneumonia After Grim Battle for His Life by Three Doctors; Unconscious Since Midnight Tuesday; Had Little Power of Resistance.'

The first I had known of Archie's illness was the night before, when I arrived in Prince Albert to visit Shirley Dawn. Mrs. Winters, who had come to meet me at the train, told me that Archie's condition was serious. I decided to go immediately from the station to the hospital, but Mrs. Winters said she had phoned before leaving the suite and was told that Archie was asleep and was resting well. This was encouraging, so I thought it best to wait and go to him the next day, but, as you see, the next day was too late. Archie was dead. At first I couldn't believe that this could be true, for I knew the man's strength, his endurance in the face of the hardships that life in the outdoors demanded. I saw him falter only once, when the shrapnel wound in his foot became inflamed as he went in search of McGinty and McGinnis. I don't remember what I intended saying, but only minutes after I heard about Archie, I phoned Dr. Lee. When I told him who was calling, he asked, 'Why in Heaven's name didn't you come as soon as you heard that Archie was ill?' I told him why. Then, greatly agitated, the doctor informed me that Archie, before he had gone into a coma – one from which he never regained consciousness – had been asking for me, urging them to send for me, saying that I was either at Great Bear Lake or at Goldfields in northern Alberta. If only I had gone to the hospital that night!

On April 14, 1938, the day after Archie's death, the story below appeared in the North Bay *Nugget*.

GREY OWL WAS ENGLISH, NOT INDIAN SAYS GUIDE

North Bay, Ont., April 14 – Grey Owl, famous Indian naturalist, who died yesterday at Prince Albert, Sask., was an

Englishman and no Indian at all, in the opinion of William H. Guppy of Timagami station.

Guppy said today he knew Grey Owl as Archie Belaney in 1906. When he enlisted with the Canadian forces in 1914, Grey Owl used the name of Archie Belaney. He said he was part Indian. The young Englishman, intensely interested in woodcraft, was taken to Timagami by Guppy who taught him to be a guide. He spoke no Indian.

'He was English' Guppy repeated. 'He spoke with an ordinary English accent – a cockney accent we used to say in those days. He learned to be a guide in very short order. He was simply full of it.'

Following the war Guppy said Belaney visited Timagami several times around 1922.

'The next thing I knew he was Grey Owl' he related. 'We have watched with interest and amusement his career as a writer and lecturer. But we will never forget him as the young Englishman whom we liked very much.'

This statement resounded around the world, and the glowing obituaries were replaced by sensational headlines: Grey Owl, the impostor of the century; the modern Bluebeard; the magnificent fake; the greatest impostor in literary history; Grey Owl, fraud, hoax, etc.

I thought of the worries, the near-starvation that we'd gone through after he quit the trap-line, of his writing and lecturing, of all the time and effort he'd put forth towards conserving wildlife, and it was awful to think that it was all for nothing. Archie's public felt they'd been gypped and that he had only been after the fast buck. This wasn't true, for a great part of the money he had made was spent in furthering his conservation ideas – his two films alone had cost $40,000. Archie had not only given his earnings, he had given his very life. He knew what price he was paying, in health, for his work, for he'd told a reporter in Ontario that another month of lecturing would kill him. A month and a day later he was dead.

One never reads of a full-blooded Englishman, Swede, or German writing this or that or having said such and such, but everything that Archie did was preceded by 'full-blooded Indian'. Even in Montreal, where he had made his first 'city' speech and where he was then practically unknown, the paper's

179

headline had featured the 'full-blooded' bit. The more Archie did, the more Indian he became in the eyes of the public, and he went along with it and became more Indian than Tecumseh himself. One may as well go the limit should it happen to facilitate the job at hand. Think what it must have cost Archie to go to his homeland, as an Indian, to plead his cause, and this in the glare of the footlights. But then, he did say he'd do anything if he thought it would make people listen to what he had to say, and he did. He also said, 'If a man believes in himself without conceit, puts everything of which he is capable into a project, and carries on in absolute sincerity of purpose, he can accomplish nearly any reasonable aim.'

Never once did I suspect that Archie was anything but what he said he was, Scotch and Indian, born in Mexico. But the instant I read that Archie was English, I remembered what he had said: 'This is going to be my last book. . . . it's about me – things that even you don't know, and will never know, at least not from me. . . .'

It's a pity he didn't live to write his *Devil in Deerskins*; he would have squared himself with the public.

In the beginning, the title of this story was to be *Grey Owl and I,* but as the story unfolded, there was, unfortunately, more about myself than there was about Archie, so, appropriately enough, I decided to call it *Devil in Deerskins.*

With his vivid and exceptional imagination, Archie would weave interesting and exciting stories around small things. I enjoyed listening to these stories and he enjoyed telling them. It was a form of entertainment and we both knew that that was what it was. One night, in a reminiscent mood, he told me of his ranch.

'My father sent me a miniature Mexican ranch – I was about five at the time. I thought it the most wonderful thing in the world, and it was. It had the little adobe houses, stables, and carved wooden horses – they had Navajo blankets instead of saddles on their backs, and little Mexican figures. Two of these figures I picked out as being my father and me, and I used to spend hour upon hour moving them about, imagining that he and I were working together on our ranch. Later, when I was able to read, I got hold of a book about Mexico and found that the hacienda, as they're called there, was absolutely authentic, right down to the little rawhide water buckets. . . .'

Another subject that he used to make up stirring stories about was a tea chest.

'My grandmother,' he would begin, 'had a tea chest that she treasured beyond anything else. It was a beautifully carved thing, of black wood, with four bowed legs. I guess it held about three or four pounds of tea. It wasn't just an ornament, for it was still in use. . . . Grandmother never allowed anyone to touch it, so each time tea was being made, Grandma had to be there because only she had the key. It must have been the way she went about bringing the key out from somewhere in the folds of her dress, and then unlocking the chest, measuring out the tea, re-locking the chest and then returning the key to its hidden place that made such an impression on me, for I had the notion that she'd been performing a religious ritual of great importance. So, when the key mysteriously disappeared one day, I all but went out of my head, for I thought that Grandma would never again have her tea, and she was sure to die. I remember burying my head in her lap and howling like hell and telling her that if she died I would die too. I only stopped when she told me the tea didn't matter, but she was sorry about losing the key to her precious chest.'

Though he said little of her, Archie thought a great deal of his Aunt Carrie.

'Aunt Carrie was always kind and affectionate. She never went stomping about, breathing fire and all that crap like Aunt Ada. Still, for all her apparent timidity, she had guts, for she often came to my rescue when Aunt Ada was pulling her stuff. . . .'

Paradoxically, when Archie was saying his worst about Miss Ada Belaney, he was at the same time unintentionally revealing a most remarkable woman. But she made a mistake, and who doesn't, when she over-indulged her vanity by attempting to turn her nephew into a super-being. Her approach to that end was much too severe, and as Archie said, 'She only succeeded in making a devil out of me.' By this, he meant that he had made it a point to do the exact opposite of what she had taught him. For example, he had consciously or unconsciously chosen a way of life that required no education, and it seemed until he began to write that Miss Belaney's work had been a waste of time.

For years he wouldn't touch a piano, which his aunt had laboured so to teach him. When he eventually did go back to the piano, it was to pound out, with great gusto, jigs, reels, etc., and never the classics. (Those were the times when he wished his aunt could see him.)

Archie detested restrictions of any description and continually flirted on the edge of law and order; at times he went a little further and crossed the line. Another thing that put Archie to work was pomp and ceremony at the table. When Archie spotted someone who, he suspected, came not to eat and make merry, but only to display his cultural upbringing and impeccable table manners, he would immediately put strategy to work and would manoeuvre in such a way that in the end the pompous unfortunate would make a *faux pas*. Archie, of course, would be the first to offer some word of sympathy, thus attracting everyone's attention to what would very likely have gone unnoticed.

People with superiority complexes were another of Archie's pet aversions, and he enjoyed nothing better than knocking the props from under them. The following is an example.

Mr. X. was the reeve, or, rather, the whole council, including constable, of a town in Ontario. He was the top man, bar none. He also owned the store where Archie bought his supplies; therefore they knew each other quite well and used to split the odd bottle in Mr. X.'s office at the back of the store. However, Mr. X. was afflicted with a giant-sized superiority complex. Archie found his condescending manner insufferable and was only waiting for the chance to cut him down to size. This chance came one afternoon when Mr. X. happened to be in a mood to imbibe a little more recklessly than usual. Archie was all wheels himself, but was alert enough to realize that this was what he had been waiting for. He also realized that he needed a little time to think, to plan. It didn't take him long.

'Mr. X.,' he said, 'you are a big man in this town. In fact, you are the biggest man I have ever had the pleasure to have a drink with.'

Mr. X., carried away by all this flattery, said, 'Quite so, quite so. Have another drink, Archie.'

'Say, I just got a hell of a good idea,' said Archie, taking the drink and continuing. 'We're having a trout supper at the house. If you would care to honour me with your presence, you'd make me the happiest man in the world.'

'A trout supper, you say?' Archie confirmed this. 'That's my favourite dish! I'll be there, Archie.'

Of course, Archie hadn't the faintest idea what Mrs. B. at the boarding house was going to serve for supper, but he'd said fish, so fish it was going to be. Now he needed to go to the store – he had only to walk through the door to get there – so he said, 'Excuse me, a moment, Mr. X., but I've just run out of snuff.'

Mr. X. said 'O.K.' Archie never used snuff.

At the store he ordered half a dozen large lake trout. If Mr. X. was going to have fish, everybody was going to have fish. Then he called to one of the boys who was hanging about the store and asked him to take the bag of trout to his boarding house, instructing him to tell the cook to boil the fish and have it ready by six o'clock. That done, Archie thought it best to take Mr. X. home before he changed his mind. Though Mrs. B. had never met Mr. X., she was quite aware of who he was, and she certainly never expected he would ever enter her humble abode, so when she saw him coming through the door, her arms flew up – she was overcome. It was like having the king of England dropping in unexpectedly.

Archie endeavoured to entertain his guest as best he could. He played the piano and poured some drinks and then he played the piano and poured some more, and on it went. By the time supper was ready, they were pretty high. At last they were seated at the table with the rest of the boarders and dinner was served. Mr. X., in joyous anticipation, lifted a forkful of food to his mouth, but it was at this point that Archie gasped and exclaimed in mock horror, 'No, no! Mr. X., we never, never eat boiled fish with a fork!'

'Oh, I didn't know. . . .'

'Of course you didn't,' said Archie, magnanimously, and added, helpfully, 'Just hoist 'er up with the good old hooks, Mr. X., and dig in.'

To the delight of the others, Mr. X. picked up the fish and 'dug in'. Later, Archie, confiding to a friend, said, 'It's funny, but Mr. X.'s condescending manner towards me has, mysteriously, disappeared.'

There is another episode about Archie and Mr. X. This happened long before the fish story.

One lonely afternoon, Archie, having a few drinks, felt in need of company, so he called on Bill. His pal wasn't in, but it didn't take much imagination to figure out where Bill would be. Bill and the wife of a friend of Archie's were having an affair. Archie felt sorry for the husband, but he didn't know what to do about it; he'd dismissed the thought of going right over and giving Bill a talking to, because that might start a fight and attract much unwanted attention to the goings-on. However, Archie thought he could at least throw Bill a hint, so he went for his axe and marched right over to his friend's house, where Bill was. As it happened, in preparation for a new foundation, the building was propped upon wooden pilings. Archie chose the prop under the bedroom floor and started swinging the axe. So preoccupied was he with the job at hand that he didn't hear a door open and someone leave the house. Suddenly he was startled out of his wits by a thunderous roar from behind.

'Archie!' came the voice of Mr. X., now in the capacity of the town constable. Archie, knowing that voice only too well, stood up and with all the innocence of one cultivating his little old garden patch said 'Yes sir?' Owing to his many encounters in previous years, Archie knew that the 'Yes sir?' approach was the quickest way of getting out of a tight spot.

'Come!' ordered Mr. X. ominously.

Archie followed the man to his office.

'Sit down!' said the scowling Mr. X., pointing to a chair.

'Yes sir,' said Archie, dropping to the chair. Mr. X. coughed. Archie jumped nervously and said 'Yes, sir.'

'Yes, what? I didn't say a damned word,' barked the man, impatiently.

'Yes, sir,' from Archie again.

'Archie,' began the long-suffering Mr. X., 'I had hoped – no – I had come to believe that the years had simmered you down. I even thought that the war had knocked some sense into you. Tell me, why do you go chopping people's houses down?'

'Yes, sir,' murmured Archie.

'Oh, for heaven's sake, shut up! You and your phoney yes

184

sir, yes sir. . . .' He was about to lash out again when Archie, with a great show of repentance, interrupted.

'Pul-lease, Mr. X., I've had all I can take; I can't take any more. I know how wrong I was. . . . I don't know what flew into me. . . . I'm all shooken up.' He then, calmly, lifted a flask from his hip and with a Satanic grin said, 'Excuse me, sir, but do you happen to have a glass?'

'Yes, as a matter of fact, Archie, I happen to have two glasses,' replied Mr. X. with a wink.

In Montreal, one January, when he went to see a specialist about his foot, Archie met a fellow in a bar who said he was an aristocrat and had been a captain in the British army. Hudder, as I will call him, was in a bad way – hung-over, bumming drinks, and his wife had left him. Archie, an old soldier, soon remedied the hangover bit, but he was hardly able to do anything about the wife, except to listen sympathetically to Hudder's long, sad story. In the end, Archie invited Hudder to return with him to Bisco and go trapping. Having accepted the invitation, Hudder confessed he wore neither shoes or socks under his rubbers and spats, and that he wore a 'foul' pair of pyjamas as underwear.

So, full of joviality and schnapps, they left the bar and went to a shop where Hudder was outfitted with suitable clothes for the woods. Next on the agenda was to retrieve Hudder's spectacles and dental plate from a pawn shop and get a supply of spirits for the long journey west. Sorry to say, but they'd no sooner got into the bush than Hudder, without alcohol, became disagreeable – antagonistic. Archie tried to ignore it, but Hudder went too far when he said the Canadian army was nothing more than an armed mob. Years later Archie described how he got even with Hudder:

'I was happier than a toad in hell when spring came and we were in Bisco again. . . . We'd split the profits of the hunt, and I fully expected Hudder to take off like a shot, but he didn't. When I met him, a week later, he told me that his wife was on her way to be with him. I thought it would be nice if we gave her a reception befitting the occasion – the reconciliation of the estranged couple; to be honest, I was looking for a little excitement. I rounded up a bunch of friends, both Indian and white, and told them that a very important personage was coming to town and this was our chance to show the world that Bisco was a place to be remembered. They said they'd enjoy a hullabaloo too. The idea was to get a war-dance going; we had the necessary regalia, because we'd done it before, for our own amusement of course. When everything was all set to go, I went to Hudder and told him we were putting on a shindig in his honour, and if his wife cared to see a little local colour, she would be welcome.

'On the night of the show, we made a big bonfire by the edge of the bush and had an area lined off for the spectators, who were coming in droves. When the Hudders arrived, the "savages" filed out from the trees to the beat of drums, and, with voices low, they circled the fire and faded into the background. Then, the heap big chief – that was me – appeared out of the shadows and began with the speech. Amidst the snickering, heckling, and wahoos, I told them we had a thief, who had committed the dastardly deed of stealing from a friend, and he was now to be tortured and burnt at the stake. Then, the prisoner, in his combination underwear and G string, was dragged out of the bush and tied to the stake.

'With the exception of those with drums, we were armed with knives, spears, tomahawks, and bottles of ketchup, which we splashed on the "captive". With all that uproar, nobody noticed the ketchup bottles, and they thought the prisoner was bleeding to death. Judging from the howls of the poor devil, I guess some of us got too close to him with the fire-brands – it was either that or he was a hell of a good actor. Anyway, women started to scream and faint all over the place, and the men yelled and cursed; a fellow shouted, "Cut that out, you crazy pack of bastards!" Then someone wired to Sudbury, saying that there was a massacre going on in Bisco.'

Archie had often said, 'My aunt succeeded only in making a devil out of me. . . .' I wonder if he ever blamed her for the 'massacre' and for his many other escapades? After he started writing, he never once said a disparaging word about Miss Ada Belaney. In fact, he dedicated his first book *The Men of the Last Frontier* to her. The dedication read as follows.

Dedicated as a tribute to my Aunt whom I must thank for such education that enables me to interpret into words the spirit of the forest, beautiful for all its underlying wildness.

The controversy about Archie's origin went on relentlessly in the weeks after his death. If by this time I had any ideas left about Archie being from Mexico, they were thoroughly shaken when I read the newspaper account of his mother's letter to Miss Ada Belaney (who was her sister-in-law, not her sister as the newspaper said).

GREY OWL'S 'MOTHER' WRITES TO SISTER ON FAMOUS 'SON'S' DEATH

London, April 21 [1938] – The British Press today continued to interest itself in Grey Owl, the naturalist who died last week in Saskatchewan where he made his home. The question is whether he was an Indian half-breed, as he himself maintained,* or Archibald Belaney, Englishman, with no Indian blood.

Latest development is a letter published in the *News Chronicle* as one sent by Belaney's mother from Devon to her sister at Hastings.

'I write with regret of the passing of my beloved son' the letter said. 'It is the passing of a great man with a soul so unique that never has there been another like him.'

When, finally, I was convinced that Archie was English, I had the awful feeling for all those years I had been married to a ghost, that the man who now lay buried at Ajawaan was someone I had never known, and that Archie had never really existed.

Not all of the newspapers were concerned with Archie's background:

What, after all, does his ancestry matter? The essential facts about his life are not in dispute, for as conservation officer under the Canadian Government, and as lecturer and Broadcaster in Great Britain, he worked unceasingly for the protection of wild life. This work, and, in particular, his efforts

*L. Dickson, Archie's good friend and publisher, was so convinced that Archie was part Indian that in July, 1938, he asked me to England expressly to meet Mrs. Scott-Brown, Archie's mother, hoping that I would, or could, detect in her a drop of Indian blood. Of course, there wasn't a trace.

187

on behalf of the beaver colonies in Canada, gained him the popular title of 'ambassador from the wild'. When a man has devoted his best years to such a cause it is surely unfair that he should be dubbed an 'imposter' because he may, if certain evidence is correct, have been an Englishman and not a Red Indian. Those who have read Grey Owl's books or heard his broadcasts cannot doubt his sincerity, and the record of his work speaks for itself. In these circumstances it would seem that Grey Owl should be accepted for the nature-lover which he undoubtedly was, and that controversy over his ancestry may be dismissed as unnecessary gossip. (Liverpool *Daily Post,* April 21, 1938.)

The trapper turned author and became a best-seller, known and loved the world over. His easy success embarrassed him. He felt some shame at coining money by the easy expedient of publishing his notes on his hobby and life interest. He continued to feel a certain claustrophobia when his vast public demanded his presence in the great cities of the Old World to lecture. His books, often autobiographical, have a powerful charm, like Thompson Seton's. They were written not for the scientific, but for the general public, but they reveal the accuracy of his powers of observation. His love of the wild and his simple style give them atmosphere all the time. His writings are the *locus classicus* for the beaver. The man who killed so many wild creatures came to loathe killing and blood sports. I believe that success neither spoiled him nor his pleasure in wild life. (*The Sphere,* April 30, 1938.)

The world is ready to forget the private lives of Burns, Shelley, Byron, Marlowe, Verlaine, Swinburn, Rossetti. The beauty of their work lives on.
So it should be with Grey Owl. He preached a gospel of tolerance towards the animal world, not for sentimental reasons, but because, as he said, 'It is just sense.'
He will be freely extended the tolerance he preached by all who remember with gratitude that he was a man who had the courage to tell the civilized world that it still had much to learn. (*Daily Herald,* April 21, 1938.)

I didn't go to Archie's funeral because Yvonne Perrier, who Archie had married in 1937, was then in hospital in

Regina, Saskatchewan, and therefore unable to attend. So, the last time I saw Archie was when I left Beaver Lodge. (I did not marry while Archie was alive, because a divorce is unknown among the Lac Simon Indians, and I considered Papati's marriage ceremony legally binding. It wasn't until December 2, 1939, that Count Eric Moltke Huitfeldt, of Sweden, and I were married.)

Archie was buried at Ajawaan Lake, as was his desire. His grave was marked with a simple soldier's cross, indicating 'A. Belaney' horizontally, and 'Grey Owl' vertically.

Below is an excerpt from his first book *The Men of the Last Frontier*, which tells of the deep significance of his acquisition of the name Grey Owl.

Many years ago I cast my lot in with that nation known under the various appellations of Chippeways, Algonquins, Londucks, and Ojibways. A blood-brother proved and sworn, by moose-head feast, wordless chant, and ancient ritual was I named before a gaily decorated and attentive concourse, when Ne-ganik-abo, 'Man-that-stands-ahead,' whom none living remember as a young man, danced the conjuror's dance beneath the spruce trees, before an open fire; danced the ancient steps to the throb of drums, the wailing of reed pipes, and the rhythmical skirring of turtle shell rattles; danced alone before a sacred bear-skull set beneath a painted rawhide shield, whose bizarre device might have graced the tomb of some long-dead Pharaoh. And as the chanting rose and fell in endless reiteration, the flitting shadows of his weird contortions danced a witches' dance between the serried tree-trunks. The smoke hung in a white pall short of the spreading limbs of the towering trees, and with a hundred pairs of beady eyes upon me, I stepped out beneath it when called on. And not one feral visage relaxed in recognition, as, absorbed in the mystery of their ritual, they intoned the almost forgotten cadences. 'Hi-Heeh, Hi-Heh, Ho! Hi-Heh, Hi-Heh, Ha! Hi-Hey, Hi-Hey, Ho! Hi-Ho, Hi-Ho, Ha!' And on and on in endless repetition, until the monotony of the sounds had the same effect on the mind that the unvarying and measured markings of a snake have on the eye. The sensation of stepping into a motionless ring was that of suddenly entering a temple, devoted to the worship of some pagan deity, where the walls were lined with images cast in bronze; and there

I proudly received the name they had devised, which the old man now bestowed upon me.

At that the drums changed their rhythm and the whole assemblage, hitherto so still, commenced to move with a concerted, swaying, rocking motion, in time to the thunder of the drums, and the circle commenced to revolve about me. The chant broke into a series of rapidly ascending minor notes, which dropped from the climax to the hollow, prolonged hoot of the Owl, whose name I now bore.